Take
Charge
Now

A Woman's Guide to Personal
and Family Finance

Take Charge Now

A Woman's Guide to Personal
and Family Finance

Patricia Lovett-Reid

KEY PORTER BOOKS

Canadian Cataloguing in Publication Data

Lovett-Reid, Patricia

    Take charge now: a woman's guide to personal and family finance

ISBN 1-55263-110-9

1. Women – Finance, Personal.   2. Finance, Personal – Psychological aspects.
3. Women – Psychology.   I. Title.

HG179.L686   1999   332.024'042   C99-931510-2

THE CANADA COUNCIL | LE CONSEIL DES ARTS
FOR THE ARTS | DU CANADA
SINCE 1957 | DEPUIS 1957

The publisher gratefully acknowledges the support of the Canada Council for the Arts and the Ontario Arts Council for its publishing program.

Canada

We acknowledge the financial support of the Government of Canada through the Book Publishing Industry Development Program (BPIDP) for our publishing activities.

Key Porter Books Limited
70 The Esplanade
Toronto, Ontario
Canada M5E 1R2

www.keyporter.com

Electronic formatting: Jean Lightfoot Peters
Design: Peter Maher

Printed and bound in Canada

99 00 01 02 03 6 5 4 3 2 1

Table of Contents

Acknowledgements   vii

Preface   ix

Chapter 1: Six Mistakes   1

Chapter 2: Quiz   13

Chapter 3: Getting Started   20

Chapter 4: Learn More and Earn More   55

Chapter 5: Maxing Out Your Investments   93

Acknowledgements

This book was created with the wisdom and assistance of many people.

We are deeply grateful to all the women we have met in speaking engagements across the country. We appreciate their honesty and frankness in sharing with us the experiences that formed the basis and the inspiration for this book.

On a personal note, our involvement in this book has been an extremely rewarding endeavour. We shared a lot as women and could relate to the many struggles and successes expressed so honestly by those we hope will read and learn from this book. The feedback and guidance they provided to ensure we were addressing the issues most critical to their own experiences contributed immensely to the book.

We would like to thank J. Mark Wettlaufer, President, TD Asset Management Inc., for his continuous commitment to and belief in the Women in the KNOW program. In addition, we would like to thank the Bank's executive for their support of this initiative: Charlie Baillie, Allen Bell, Bob Kelly, and Steve McDonald.

We would like to recognize the efforts of Miranda Koffski and Jennifer Stuart, who put a tremendous amount of time and expertise into ensuring our final product met their extremely high standards.

The preparation of the book required the generous help and cooperation of a number of TD Bank colleagues, in particular Bill Bennett, Elaine Blades, Nicholas Chan, Edna Chu, Marilyn Kumabe, Zora Milovanov, Jessica Mossman, Jane Stubbington, Diane Tsirlis and Tim Watson.

Our gratitude is further extended to our associates at TD Asset Management who provided insightful suggestions: Ann Marie Beuerman, Sandy Cimoroni, Dave Curtis, Cindy Denwood, Angela Dickins, Samantha Deutsch, Angell Kasparian, Cathy Marcoccia, Bruce Shirreff, Andrew Trimble, and Susan Winmill.

We also appreciated the desire and drive to complete this project of David Holmes and Katherine Holmes of Holmes Creative Communications, whose creative talent and support we know we can always rely upon.

Thanks to Key Porter Books, especially Anna Porter for her direction and valuable input, Susan Renouf for her persistence and insight, Lorraine Kelly who supported this project from the beginning, and Diane Broad, who demonstrated considerable patience during the editing process.

In closing, it is with great pleasure that we acknowledge we are donating all the royalties of the book to The Children's Miracle Network. The mission of The Children's Miracle Network is to generate funds and awareness programs for the benefit of children served by its associated hospitals.

PATRICIA LOVETT-REID

Preface

"The perfection of wisdom, and the end of true philosophy, is to proportion our wants to our possessions, our ambitions to our capacities."
—FRANCES WRIGHT

In the fall of 1998 I had the privilege of travelling across Canada to meet hundreds of women of all ages and all backgrounds. These women attended the seminars offered by TD Asset Management Inc.'s "Women in the Know" program. Each participant wanted to learn more about getting on the road to financial security. What we discussed was achieving balance in our lives.

The success of the seminars was attributable to the women who participated. I learned so much through that experience that I believed it was worth sharing with a larger audience.

In the following pages you will meet a number of women in a wide variety of life situations. What they share in common is a desire to achieve a sense of security and a sense of direction in their lives. Our decision to write this book for women only came not from a desire to exclude men nor from a naive assumption that men are without stress and multiple responsibilities. Of course they are not. Do men not have wishes and dreams, stress and responsibilities? Of course they do. But, married or single, young or old, career women or work-at-home mothers, women are different from men. Some have even suggested that we are from different planets. By and large, women view the world differently and today, on the eve of the millennium, women have a greater need to pause and look at themselves in relation to the world.

We all know that no goal—financial, personal, work-related, or family-centred—exists in isolation. Financial security is only one component of a well-balanced life. And unless you are named as an heir in your very rich uncle's will, it takes time, focus, and clear thinking to know what you want and how to achieve it, while also working toward other goals in your life.

The fact is that most of us spend a lot of time juggling. We have work, we have home, we may have kids, we may have spouses or partners and aging parents, we have food to cook, bills to pay and, somewhere in there, we'd like a social life. Our lives are the sum of many parts, our selves a conglomerate of identities—wife, mother, daughter, sister, co-worker, friend. For many of us, the idea of focusing long enough to set a goal is preposterous. We're just trying to get through the day without a major catastrophe. So, before we even approach the subject of our financial goals, we must step back and take a careful and thoughtful look at our lives. We must determine what it is we really want.

In the early days of feminism, much time and energy was spent on male-bashing—on blaming men for suppressing women throughout the ages. Those days are, for the most part, gone. The best of what the early feminists fought for has dramatically altered the position of women in most societies. Today, women realize that they can be what they want to be, who they want to be, and still share their achievements with a husband and family. In short, they can be both June Cleaver and Gloria Steinem in the same lifetime. And so a new phenomenon emerges—Superwoman.

But, as Superwoman tries to have it all, to be the perfect everything to herself and to everyone around her, she risks burning out or doing everything only half as well as she'd like. Burnout is the sign of an unbalanced life.

We've come to believe that we can have it all. We can marry or choose not to. We can have children or choose not to. We can get an education, build a career, or choose not to. Or is all of that a fantasy too? Many of us married and discovered that it was not a permanent state. Many of us would like to stay at home with our children but can't afford to, and some of us believe that we can do and have it all, but lose our peace of mind in the process.

And so we ask the questions: Is this what I want? Have I really taken charge of my life? Or am I too tired, too busy to know? Out of all of those dilemmas, all of those choices, all of those questions, one truth emerges: I am responsible for my own health, wealth, and happiness.

What are your realities? What is your personal profile? What are your dreams? What is within your control to change? As much as we share a lot as women, each of us is different, unique in our own way. Some of us are career women, some retired, some are mothers, perhaps grandmothers, some are just starting out in relationships or careers. Some are single moms, some are part of a two-income family.

How many of us play the "if only" game? If only I won the lottery, all my financial troubles would be over. If only I could take one long relaxing vacation, I could cope. If only, if only, if only.

I believe that there are five important elements in a well-balanced life: family, friends, fitness, finance, and focus. How we serve each of these elements is a benchmark for the degree of balance in our lives. To achieve a sense of balance, we must face the reality that there are limits to our time and limits to our energy. We can only do the best we can.

Let's start with family.

A friend of mine who found herself suddenly single with two small children and a very demanding career recounts a story that she says crystallizes her experience with a busy life. Her five-year-old daughter was invited to lunch at her aunt's house and to spend the day with a four-year-old cousin. At the lunch table, her little cousin said to her stay-at-home mom, "What's for dinner?" To which her mother replied, "Spaghetti." My friend's daughter, eyes wide in astonishment, exclaimed, "You know that *now*?"

Although years later she can laugh while recounting the story, at the time, it caused a jarring pang of guilt that she wasn't doing enough for her children. But how much is enough? We can run around frantically declaring that there's never enough time for our families or we can order our lives, our schedules, and our routines to do what we can, when we can.

The next "F" is Friends. In simpler days, some women gathered in the morning over coffee, or in the afternoon over the bridge table, while the children were in school. Today we must check our daytimers to see when we can "fit in" our friends. And in a busy schedule, our friends are often the first to be sacrificed.

We who care about making everything right for everyone else often start by sacrificing the things we enjoy most. Guilt again. It's hard to tell your family that you need to spend some time with your friends. But you do. We need to unburden our lives and we need to talk. Most importantly, we need to learn to laugh at our crises and our perceived failures. The time you spend with your friends can be just as important as attending your child's soccer game.

Fitness can be a scary thing. We ignore our bodies because we don't have time for them. They are serving us well so they must be well, right? Not always. You don't have to get up at the crack of dawn to join those aerobic experts on television. If you're not a health-club kind of person, think about what type of activity you enjoy. How about strapping on those runners and getting off the bus two stops earlier? How about a walk to the store to get some milk instead of jumping in the car to go two blocks? Do you have a bottle of water in your car or in your brief-case? How about an apple instead of a chocolate bar?

And just as important as diet and exercise is attitude. Stress kills, but before it does, it makes us sick. That's reality. Love it or hate it, we've only got one body and it will hold out as long as we take care of it. Simple changes can make a huge difference in our well-being. When you're under stress, take deep breaths, eat well, and remember what your mother told you: "Things will look better in the morning." Remember: a good night's sleep can help reduce stress, or help you to better handle it.

Finances. The fourth F word. Whether we like it or not, money does make the world go 'round. And, although it may not buy happiness, the lack of it can cause great unhappiness. That's simply our reality. How do we balance the need to make and save money with all of the other elements in our lives? I think the phrase "financial health" is a good place to start.

What is "health" in terms of your finances? Can you take care of your finances in the same way you take care of your body? Yes, if your life has balance. If you ignore making important decisions about your finances, you might suffer some of the same consequences as if you ignore your body's needs.

We all recognize that we must save for our retirement. Women tend to live longer than men and we're all living longer than our grandparents did. Many of us could have possibly 30 or more years of retirement to prepare for. And of course, in the meantime, we have our children's education to think about, perhaps a mortgage to take care of, and that great North American pastime, accumulating stuff.

Part of the exercise of achieving balance in our lives involves taking stock of what we really want, and all of that "stuff" is a big part of it. When you examine your personal profile, when you look at the elements of your life—family, friends, fitness, finances, and focus—a large part of that exercise is asking yourself, What do I really want? What will give me peace of mind? And in going through that exercise, we must balance what we want or need today versus what we know we will need in the future.

You've heard the expression, "When the going gets tough, the tough go shopping." Many of us know that when we're feeling low, it feels good to get more stuff. But it's just a short-term solution. A great new pair of shoes may lift your heels and your spirits, but is that what you really want? Compare that feeling to paying off your credit card, making an extra mortgage payment, or watching your RRSP grow. Where's the long-term power? Often, we wish or worry our lives away. And that causes anxiety and sleepless nights, especially if that retirement date is looming in your future.

Finally, Focus. The ability, courage, and resolute purpose to focus on both immediate and future priorities is a challenge we all face. When our lives become frantic, we can so easily become "me-centred," focusing on everything we are not doing right and feeling overwhelmed. Yet, the feeling of liberation that comes from knowing what you're doing in an orderly, organized manner is priceless. The value is virtually immeasurable. The barrier to entry, so to speak, is fairly simple: Will you or won't you take the time to gain control over your investment in *you*?

Ask yourself: What do I really want? Perhaps, more importantly, what do I have that I value, that gives me strength, joy, and pride in myself? Where can I find the strength I need to act, to make decisions, to make choices?

Family, Friends, Fitness, Finances, and Focus. Sources of anxiety or sources of strength. To transform those elements in our lives into sources of strength requires real determination. We must stand back and look at ourselves. We must ask ourselves if we are making wise and reasoned choices or are just being swept along in the current of life.

To focus on ourselves is not a selfish act. In giving to ourselves, we gain the strength to achieve what we must and balance to achieve what we want.

The women whose stories are recounted in this book are composites of the many women I met from coast to coast. We also had some fun with the book because, despite the fact that life is a very serious business, humour is a critical element in any healthy life.

And in this book, we have concentrated on achieving *financial* health through a step-by-step process that we hope will be helpful to women at many ages and stages in life. Whether you find yourself overwhelmed by financial matters and unable to create order from your financial chaos, or whether you're doing fairly well financially and would like some sound advice on how to progress to the next level, we think you'll find some practical solutions here. And once you feel your financial life is under control, it is likely that the other pressures you're experiencing may diminish.

I hope that within these pages readers will be stimulated to discuss their anxieties and fears, find some practical solutions to their financial challenges, and move a step closer to realizing what we all long for: peace of mind.

PATRICIA LOVETT-REID
Managing Director
Women in the Know

1 Six Mistakes

Faulty Thinking, Wrong Assumptions, and Major Regrets

The six big financial mistakes women make

1. My plan to be happy and content with a secure future is to marry well.

> *"Diamonds are a girl's best friend."*
> —Marilyn Monroe in "Gentlemen Prefer Blondes," a song by Leo Robin

And they both lived happily ever after.

Marriage is a great thing. It provides love and comfort. Children and grandchildren. Emotional and financial stability.

Or that's what many of us are led to believe.

And why wouldn't we?

The happily-ever-after scenario played out in every hit movie is always girl-gets-boy and, by no coincidence, boy is rarely poor. So many of us believed Marilyn Monroe when she told us that "diamonds are a girl's best friend."

Perhaps you could argue that women don't think like that anymore. You say that was another time—a time when women were expected to marry, have children, stay home, play bridge, cook meals, and be a great hostess.

But is that time really behind us? We'd all like to believe that women have made great strides, embraced independence, taken their rightful place in the job market, and are now facing a happy and financially secure future.

We'd like to believe it and certainly some women have achieved it. But some of us haven't. As long as the myth of marrying for love and money prevails, many of us will continue to believe in it. It worked for Marilyn in the fifties. It worked for Audrey Hepburn in *Breakfast at Tiffany's*. And it really worked for Julia Roberts in *Pretty Woman*.

But what happens after happily-ever-after? Reality. Nearly half of all marriages end in divorce. That means single women, with or without children, are on their own, trying to make a living. Not many movies come to mind about terrified women who dive into the job market inexperienced and unprepared.

We all have our fantasies. But putting your financial life and health on hold while you wait for Prince Charming is not only highly unlikely to result in a happy ending, it's also a fairly good indicator that your priorities are out of whack.

The best way to find the right person is to be busy getting on with your own life. Then, with a clear head, you can decide to marry him because you love him, marry him because you're friends, marry him because you're great partners who'll make and manage the money together. Marry a man, not a bankroll.

What if you do enjoy a long, successful relationship? What if you do live happily ever after? And many women do. Will you outlive your husband? Statistics say it's likely you will. And what will happen then? Many women find themselves dealing not only with the grief and loss that comes with losing their husband but also with the dizzying confusion of the family finances. Let me tell you about Elizabeth.

She and her husband Richard had just begun enjoying his retirement after a long and successful career. They golfed together, enjoyed a wide circle of friends, and a large family including five children and nine grandchildren. Then Richard died suddenly of a massive heart attack.

Elizabeth was devastated at losing her lover, her friend, her companion. But that was only the beginning. As she sat in her beautiful suburban home, looking out on the gardens she and Richard had lovingly created together, her friend Ruth suggested that the two of them plan a winter vacation. Elizabeth said she didn't think she could do that.

"I don't know if I can afford it," she explained. "I don't know if I have to sell the house and the car. I don't know where the money is." Richard had always done well, had always given Elizabeth a generous allowance and a major credit card, but Elizabeth had neither seen nor paid a bill during her entire marriage.

She didn't even have a bank account. And now, in the midst of her mourning, she was paralyzed with fear, not knowing what to do or how to do it. Her perfect marriage had come to an end and now she was on her own, forced to start, at age 64, to understand the meaning of financial health.

With the help of family and friends, Elizabeth found a good financial planner and is now learning the basics of managing her money. She admits that even though Richard liked being the provider and looking after things, her big mistake had been her lack of involvement. The pain of her loss was intensified by her ignorance and the fear that gripped her at the most critical time in her life.

"I remember thinking in the middle of Richard's funeral, 'How will I pay for all of this?' Yet, all that anxiety was so unnecessary. It was so ironic. Richard wanted to take care of me and I liked it that way. But when he died, I discovered I could barely function without him."

A happy marriage is a wonderful gift, but it too requires balance. Sharing in a marriage should not be limited to the rewards of children, a home, friends, interests. A balanced marriage includes sharing both the responsibilities and the burdens. A strong union is only as strong as the individuals who share in it.

2. When I need to get away from life's disappointments I go shopping.

"I did not have 3000 pairs of shoes, I had 1060."
—Imelda Marcos

Some people shop because they need to purchase something. Other people shop because they need to shop. Shopoholics shop like alcoholics drink—too much and for the wrong reasons. Veteran shoppers report that they get a real buzz from shopping—almost an acquisition high.

After all, can we really believe that Imelda Marcos just happened to like shoes?

Many shoppers report the post-purchase anxiety they experience when the high passes, asking themselves, "Did I really need this? Do I even like this?" And some, like "I Love Lucy's" Lucy Ricardo, deal with the guilt by stashing away their purchase until enough time passes and the new unneeded purchase becomes "this old thing."

Even though the gender roles and responsibilities of men and women are blurring, we are still the shoppers. We have all kinds of reasons why we have to shop.

The excuses we make to ourselves are endless: "I really needed it," "I didn't have a thing to wear," "I deserve a treat once in a while," "I was depressed."

But few of us ask, "Can I afford this? Will this really make me feel better? What's really bothering me?"

Let's go shopping with Mary. What are we looking for? Mary doesn't know. She just wants to go shopping. Armed with all the major credit cards, we start at the mall. There are several clothing stores there and the new fall line is out.

It's only August and Mary is still wearing summer clothes. But the fall colours look so lush and she really can't recall what's in her closet from last year. So, she buys the red sweater and black skirt. She hadn't planned on buying much today but there seem to be bargains everywhere.

Her credit card is getting warm from overactivity. Although she doesn't really need any make-up, a special bonus gift is being offered to customers who buy something else. So, Mary buys a new face cream, a tan-coloured eyeshadow, and a set of make-up brushes. She drops the "free" gift into her shopping bag. As she leaves the mall, Mary picks up two new CDs and John Grisham's latest novel in hardcover. Because it's too late to go grocery shopping, Mary stops at the deli and picks up some prepared meals and a Danish chocolate cake.

Entering her apartment, loaded down with her purchases, Mary begins to unpack her treasures. She puts the make-up and the free gift in the large cupboard in the bathroom with the other make-up and free gifts. She stores the deli meal in the fridge between the leftover deli meals from Thursday and Friday and then unwraps the red sweater and black skirt. She slides open the door to her closet and pushes the hangers of summer clothes to one side. She hangs up the skirt and sweater, beside the other red sweater and black skirt, and comments, "No wonder I liked this outfit. I bought the same thing in January."

Most things in life that are bad for us are just good things gone wrong. There's nothing wrong with shopping unless it becomes your life's work. When shopping is a substitute for something else lacking in our lives, it's time to take a hard look and perhaps ask a few simple questions: Is this purchase in my budget (assuming, of course, that you have a budget)? Do you plan a shopping day or is it a compulsive activity to cover up anxiety about a bigger issue? Is it a pleasant experience or does the post-shopping guilt outweigh the fun?

Plan your purchase in advance. Think carefully about what you really need and make a list before you leave. If you're going clothes shopping, check out your wardrobe first. What do you really need? A sweater to go with a skirt you have? A scarf that would make an old outfit look new?

Become a bargain hunter. Some of the best furniture ever made ends up at auction, in second-hand stores, or at garage sales. Gently used clothing stores offer designer clothes in excellent condition for ridiculously low prices. If you want to buy retail, be an off-season shopper. Buy winter clothes in January, summer clothes in August.

Get organized. If you know what you have and what you need, you'll spend less. Do an inventory of your kitchen cupboards and refrigerator. Plan your meals around what you have. Make take-out a special treat, not an eating habit.

Check your bank balance, your credit card balance, and your budget to determine exactly how much you can afford. Know how much you can spend before you spend it.

Make shopping a pleasant, guilt-free experience.

3. No time to deal with my problems today. They'll still be here tomorrow.

> *"Fiddle-dee-dee. I'll think about that tomorrow."*
> —Scarlett O'Hara in Margaret Mitchell's *Gone With the Wind*

How many of us have said, "If only I had known then what I know now?" Unlike Scarlett who fiddle-dee-deed and finagled her way through several husbands and as many properties, most of us don't get a chance to start over again. Procrastination can be very expensive.

One of life's great financial bloopers is blocking out that little voice that says, "Hey, shouldn't I be saving some money?" But we say, "I've got years ahead of me to save. I really need a vacation. I really need a new car." And that great advice Mom and Dad gave us? "Pay yourself first." Guess what? They didn't mean buy stuff. They meant take a portion of your income and put it away for your future. But who knew?

Kim is a funny, energetic optimist who loves life and can't wait to see what will happen next. Things have always gone well for her and she thinks life is just one great adventure after another. Kim believes that worrying is a complete waste of time. Her friends love her for her energy and envy her lifestyle, enjoyed on what appears to be a modest income. What they don't know is she doesn't sleep very well. Her fortieth birthday is approaching and Kim is beginning to look at her life and her empty bank account.

It's four in the morning and Kim is playing the "if only" game in her head. "If only I hadn't taken the trip to Mexico last winter. Most of it is still on my credit card. If only I hadn't cashed in my RRSPs to buy Christmas presents. I can't even remember what I bought for everybody. If only I had started saving a little when I started working, I probably would have enough to put a down payment on a condo by now. Instead, I'm stuck in this apartment for the eighteenth year in a row." After calculating that she had spent $520 a year on lottery tickets for the last 12 years, Kim nods off, vowing that tomorrow she will begin to do things differently.

Kim is not that rare. Many of us spend time procrastinating and putting off really important decisions until "tomorrow." The important thing to remember about putting things off is that every day you delay is time and money wasted. And that's so true when it comes to saving for retirement.

Here are two very important words: "compound interest." The younger you are when you start saving, the more you'll have when you're older, not just because you saved more but because the early deposits grew more. If you start saving at 25, you're miles ahead of the person who starts saving at 40. And she's miles ahead of the person who starts at 50.

Procrastination is a big, ugly word.

If you put off an oil change, your engine could seize up. If you put off seeing the dentist, you could end up with a root canal. If you put off paying your bills, you could really blow your budget and raise your stress level, and if you put off saving for your retirement, you'll be really surprised how quickly time goes by.

It doesn't even have to be painful. If you have a plan, you can still take vacations, you can still drive a car, you can even eat. You just have to sock a little bit away from every pay.

But the big issue is finding out where your life is off balance. What is it that makes us think, "Tomorrow is another day"? Why do we put off until tomorrow what we know we should be doing today?

We're so caught up in our family, our career, our love life, our need to live for today that we often think tomorrow can wait until we deal with what's really important. Bingo. What's really important is our whole, balanced life—our todays and our tomorrows.

Scarlett O'Hara was right. Tomorrow is another day but it's one more day that you didn't save for the big tomorrow. And it's one more day that we suffer the anxiety of not dealing with that future that looms in front of us.

Planning for tomorrow is a fundamental principle of a balanced life.

You've heard the expression, "You do the math." The math of retirement savings is very simple. The longer you postpone, put it off, procrastinate, the less money you will have if Rhett Butler walks away... or never turns up.

4. So what if I don't have any money? I've got credit!

> *"Ben, I want to say one word to you—Just one word—plastics."*
> —"The Graduate" screenplay by Calder Willingham

One word. Plastic. Open your wallet and start counting. How many lovely little plastic cards do you have? Aren't they fun? When you have them, you don't need to spend your real money. You just hand over that card, slide it through, sign your name, and away you go.

We're not stupid. We really do know that we are spending money, don't we? We really do know that we have to pay when the bill comes, don't we? Sure we do.

Kathy bought a new wallet today. She had to. Her old wallet couldn't hold all her cards. She has a VISA, a MasterCard, an American Express, a card from Sears, The Bay, Zeller's, Canadian Tire, and four gas company cards. She doesn't have a lot of cash though, because by the time Kathy makes the minimum payments on all of her cards, very little cash is left. But she continues to play those games. Oh look, I don't have to pay it all. I only have to pay a tiny part of it. I'll pay the rest next month, or the month after. And there's absolutely no way I'll use the card again until I've paid it off. Well, maybe only in an emergency. Like that emergency dinner out, the emergency shoes, and the emergency trip to Florida.

Kathy is slow to learn. When card number one is maxed out, she starts on card number two. Even though she now has two bills to pay, she can afford it because she only has to pay a tiny amount on two bills. But the interest charges are growing and so are the payments. Kathy applies for another card. It's an ugly picture. Do you see it?

Kathy is in plastic prison. She realized that when she used her card to pay for an ice-cream cone. She knows that the payments on her cards are taking all of her disposable income. Once she thought she could have whatever she wanted, whenever she wanted it, but now she is starting to understand the situation. Now it's starting to hit her. It's time to face the music.

Plastic allows us to defer payment but not forever. That's why they call them credit cards. Interest rates cause debt to increase just as interest rates can increase savings. Wouldn't you prefer to watch your savings grow rather than your debt?

The next time you're tempted, try this little mantra. Say it to yourself (not out loud or else others will think you're crazy) "This is real money, this is real money."

Paying off debt is one step in a long-term financial plan. If it seems overwhelming, consider this trick invented by reformed plastic addicts. For every $25 you pay off on your credit card, put another $25 into a savings plan. It's amazing how that takes the sting out of sending them your money.

5. When I have a temporary cash-flow problem I find someone with money.

> *"I will gladly pay you Tuesday for a hamburger today."*
> —J. Wellington Wimpey

When payday seems an eternity away and you only have two loonies in your pocket, just ask your friend to loan you some money. Assure her that you'll repay her on Friday. Of course, when you receive your regular pay cheque you'll have less disposable income because you have to deduct what you owe from what you have. Or you could ask your friend if you could pay her back later when you have more money. After all, she is your friend.

When you run out of friends, go see your banker. She can offer you that great solution—the consolidation loan. That allows you to get out from under all your debts while having only one payment to make each month. It's designed to help you make a fresh start. But guess what our financially challenged friends do when they've paid off all those debts?

Let me tell you about Rachel. She was sinking in debt. She owed her parents the money they loaned her to take a computer course. She owed her friend the money she borrowed while they were on holiday together. And she owed three credit card companies the maximum balance she had racked up over the last four years.

Vowing to get out of debt, she went to see her banker. She was able to see that if she borrowed enough money from the bank to pay off everyone, she could handle the one smaller payment from the bank loan. When the loan was approved, Rachel heaved a sigh of relief. She signed the papers and left the bank. Then it hit her. No more worries about credit card balances. No more nagging from her parents. No more dirty looks from her friend. The bank had saved her and except for her loan, she didn't owe anybody anything. She couldn't believe how good that felt.

Once Rachel realized she no longer had credit card debt, she applied for a new card and said, "Yahoo, I'm going shopping." Rachel started all over again. She had fixed the problem but she hadn't changed the behaviour that got her in trouble in the first place. More debt.

Some women, like Rachel, also borrow money from themselves. Repeat this phrase, "I promise I will never cash in my RRSP to buy a couch." Savings are meant to be saved—for the long term. In fact, the government encourages us to save. When we buy an RRSP, we receive a tax deduction. On the other hand, when we cash it in, the government makes us pay tax.

Big money mistakes, like so many other things in life, are usually good things, used badly. There are plenty of good reasons to borrow money as long as you can afford to make the regular payments and as long as you view the loan as a shorter-term plan to assist in a longer-term goal. Loans, like credit cards, carry with them a promise you make to yourself and to the lender.

The obligation you sign up for is what they used to call "a matter of honour." Your lender wants to help you make a fresh start. You want to make a fresh start. You've just made a promise. It's like deciding to diet, deciding to exercise, deciding to be more tolerant with your in-laws. You've made a decision to borrow, a promise to pay back. That's the legal agreement. The strength of your soul, the sign of balance in your life, is linked to your decision to start fresh. And that means fixing what's not right. It means budgeting, changing your spending habits, looking to the future, and changing the past.

When the loan is paid, you can say, "I did it." Only you will really know how important it was.

6. I can't be bothered. I let somebody else look after my finances.

"I've always counted on the kindness of strangers."
—Blanche Dubois, Tennessee Williams' *A Streetcar Named Desire*

The days of Blanche Dubois, the fainting femme fatale who doesn't want to bother her pretty little head with complicated financial issues, may seem like ancient history. But some of us are still having a hard time taking charge of things.

If math has never been your strong suit, or even your interest, you may identify with Jill's situation.

Jill is a commercial designer, an avid reader, and not the least bit interested in money matters. She's very intelligent but when it comes to discussions around the family dinner table on the topic of compound interest rates, front-end loaded mutual funds, GICs, RRIFs, rollovers, and retirement funds, Jill yawns and usually says, "Whatever."

Jill isn't stupid. She's just not interested.

Jill and her brother inherited a considerable sum of money from their grandmother. When Jill's brother Jeff called a family meeting to discuss investment options, Jill said, "Jeff, you handle it. I have no idea what to do nor do I care."

Jill knows that her pension plan at work will pay an income after her retirement. But she doesn't know how much. She thinks she might change jobs but she's not sure what will happen to her pension. She knows she's been contributing to the Canada Pension Plan and that the government will pay her when she retires but she doesn't know how much, and she's heard that maybe by the time she retires, there won't be any more CPP. But she doesn't know why or even whether that's true.

Jill knows that she pays a lot of income tax and she's heard that there are ways to reduce that amount. But she doesn't know how and so she's done nothing. It's all so boring.

Her brother is the "financial brains" in the family. That's why, when the family inheritance came up, she left all the decisions to Jeff. Jill continued to put a bit of money in her chequing account and assumed that Jeff would look after the big stuff.

Jeff was happy to take charge. He told Jill not to worry—he'd make them a bundle.

A year later, Jill called Jeff to say she wanted her grandmother's inheritance. She had decided to leave her company and start her own design business. What she discovered was that Jeff had invested all of their money into a mining company. Unfortunately, it turned out to be "the pits."

Jill was shocked and ashamed. She's a bright, capable woman. But now, at a turning point in her life, she had no idea how she would fund her dreams. She had left "all that money stuff" to Jeff and, in doing so, Jill had given away her independence. It just never occurred to her that, with all of her artistic talent, she'd need to bother with financial trivia.

Not all of us are experts at everything and nor should we expect to be. The most common mistake we make, at any age or stage, is to assume that this is all too complicated and impossible to handle. There are many levels of financial competence. And no matter how little you think you know, you owe it to yourself to take charge of your financial future.

There are no stupid questions. Nothing must be more complicated than you want it to be. Financial advisors can walk you, step by step, through your finances to determine what you earn, how you save, what your plans and dreams are, and how you should go about achieving them.

Many, many books have been written on do-it-yourself financing or, if you're on-line, hundreds of web pages on the Internet can direct you to information with the click of a button.

You can take charge of your financial life, whatever your situation. And you can count on the kindness of strangers. Just make sure you ask the right people to help you take charge of your future.

2 Quiz

What's the State of Your Financial Health?

How you handle your finances is as unique to you as your personality, your taste in clothes, your priorities, and your opinions. Some of us know exactly where every loonie goes, making sure we get the most from our hard-earned cash. Some of us never have a clue what our bank balance is. We go to the ATM, cross our fingers, and hope there's some money left. And some of us think we're pretty good at managing money, most of the time.

Which type are you?

Do you have a savings account? A retirement plan? A will? Some mutual funds? A piggy bank? Lots of credit cards?

Let's find out.

This quiz is designed to rate the state of your financial health. Your responses to the questions will help you to determine the level of your financial thinking and the state of your financial health. Once you've done that, you can check the financial tips section to find out how you can improve your financial health right away.

Take the quiz and *be honest*. If you believe you've made some really stupid financial mistakes, don't worry, you're not alone. You *can* turn things around. Get out your pencil—and away you go.

1. Do you have life insurance?
  a) Yes
  b) No
  c) Don't know

2. **Do you have disability insurance?**
   a) Yes
   b) No
   c) Don't know

3. **Your friend is drawing up a will. You respond:**
   a) I already have a will.
   b) I should draw up a will as well.
   c) I don't need a will at this stage of my life.
   d) I don't need a will—period.

4. **An insurance agent calls and suggests that you meet to discuss your life insurance needs. You reply:**
   a) No thanks, I already have a policy.
   b) I'm single so I don't really need any right now—I'll call you when I get married and/or have children.
   c) I don't think life insurance is a necessity.

5. **Your current approach to finances could be described as:**
   a) Plan for tomorrow—you never know what life will throw your way.
   b) Try to save a little when you can.
   c) Live for today—worry about the finances tomorrow.

6. **What is the maximum amount of foreign content (non-Canadian investment) you can have in an RRSP?**
   a) 10%
   b) 20%
   c) 30%
   d) Don't know

7. **Thinking about your RRSPs, do you:**
   a) Seldom or never contribute to an RRSP
   b) Make sure you contribute something to your RRSP every year
   c) Maximize your RRSP contributions every year

8. **Which of the following carries the greatest financial risk:**
   a) Fixed-income funds
   b) Blue-chip equity funds
   c) T-bill funds
   d) Resource funds
   e) Don't know

9. **Thinking about the management of your household finances, how involved would you say you are:**
   a) Very involved
   b) Somewhat involved
   c) Not at all involved

10. **Your philosophy on credit cards is:**
    a) You are better off without them—You don't have any.
    b) The fewer cards you have the easier they are to manage.
    c) More cards means more credit, and that's the way to go.

11. **Your approach to paying your monthly bills is:**
    a) You make sure you pay off all your bills on time so you never have to pay late charges.
    b) Late charges are a fact of life—you try, but never seem to pay *all* your bills on time.
    c) You don't even think about late payment charges—you don't pay bills.

12. **In terms of your personal credit, you:**
    a) Know you have a good credit rating.

   b) Are pretty sure you have a credit rating, but have no idea what it is.

   c) Have never borrowed money or held a credit card solely in your name.

13. The "time value of money" refers to:
   a) The way lawyers and other professionals charge clients—by the hour.

   b) The daily rate at which currency exchange fluctuates.

   c) The compound interest accumulated over time.

   d) Don't know.

14. Your view on retirement is:
   a) It's never too early to start saving—and you are.

   b) You'll start saving for retirement once your finances are under control.

   c) You are too young to start thinking about retirement—let alone saving for it.

   d) You are resigned to the fact that you'll never be able to afford to retire.

15. You would describe your approach to budgeting as:
   a) You understand the need for budgeting, and take care to allocate you money accordingly.

   b) You try to budget but it's difficult to stick with it.

   c) What budget? You don't have one.

16. Your investments are:
   a) Non-existent

   b) A savings account

   c) Managed by you and consist of self-directed RRSPs and other investments

   d) Handled by a financial advisor

17. **You contribute to your financial investments:**
    a) Never—you don't have any financial investments
    b) Somewhat regularly—the amount varies according to what you think you can afford
    c) Just at tax time
    d) Monthly or quarterly via an automatic purchase plan

18. **You contribute to your savings:**
    a) Nothing—there is never anything left over
    b) Whatever you can
    c) About 5% of your after-tax income
    d) About 10% of your after-tax income

19. **How familiar are you with investing and the different types of investment products available?**
    a) Just starting to learn
    b) Know a little about mutual funds, but not in-depth
    c) Consider yourself to be fairly knowledgeable about a broad range of investments
    d) Consider yourself very knowledgeable and experienced in investments

20. **Your approach to dealing with financial surprises and emergencies can best be described as:**
    a) You'll deal with them when they happen the best way you can.
    b) You don't have a plan in place.
    c) You have set aside money to cover three to six months of expenses.
    d) You have a little money set aside, but it wouldn't cover three months worth of expenses.

SCORING:

1. a) 2 b) 0 c) 0
2. a) 2 b) 0 c) 0
3. a) 3 b) 2 c) 0 d) 0
4. a) 3 b) 1 c) 0
5. a) 3 b) 2 c) 0
6. a) 0 b) 3 c) 0 d) 0
7. a) 0 b) 1 c) 4
8. a) 0 b) 0 c) 0 d) 1 e) 0
9. a) 2 b) 1 c) 0
10. a) 0 b) 1 c) 0
11. a) 3 b) 1 c) 0
12. a) 3 b) 1 c) 0
13. a) 0 b) 0 c) 1 d) 0
14. a) 3 b) 1 c) 1 d) 0
15. a) 4 b) 1 c) 0
16. a) 0 b) 1 c) 2 d) 3
17. a) 0 b) 3 c) 2 d) 1
18. a) 0 b) 1 c) 2 d) 3
19. a) 1 b) 2 c) 3 d) 4
20. a) 0 b) 0 c) 4 d) 2

People who have a high level of financial health play an active role in managing their finances for both today and the future. They also tend to be very knowledgeable in areas relating to budgeting and investments. **If you scored on your Financial Quotient (FQ):**

20 or under *Getting Started* FQ rating: C
Oops!—Your financial health receives a failing grade. Chances are fairly good that today, your finances have more control over you than you do over them. You have quite a bit of work ahead of you, and there is no better time to start than right now.

21–39 *Learn More and Earn More* **FQ rating: B**
On the Right Track—Like many women, you recognize the importance of having control over your personal finances. You are on the right track, but you can still do a number of things to gain greater control and greater peace of mind.

40–56 *Maxing Out Your Investments* **FQ rating: A**
Congratulations!—You are already in good financial health. But don't be complacent—there is *always* room to improve your financial health.

How to Improve Your Investment in You

You've taken the quiz and you've rated yourself somewhere between "Oops!" and "Congratulations!" Perhaps you related a little too closely to some of the six big financial mistakes women make. Don't despair. Help is on the way. Or maybe you scored really well and now you'd like to learn more about increasing your investments or saving on your taxes. Read on.

The next three chapters are loaded with practical financial tips to help you get started, learn more and earn more, and maximize your investments.

You may want to proceed immediately to the chapter that corresponds to your quiz score (chapter 3 for a C score, chapter 4 for B, and chapter 5 for A), or you may want to start at the beginning and methodically work your way through.

At the end of each chapter, you'll find a checklist. Listed there are the steps to improving your financial health, starting with the basics of goals and budgeting and ending with estate planning and preparing for retirement.

As you assess your financial health, rework your financial plan, and continue to improve your financial situation, you might want to revisit the checklists to see what kind of progress you're making.

3 Getting Started

Financial Tips for Women Who Feel Overwhelmed

Your quiz score indicates that you've been putting off taking care of your financial health. You know that you must address it but you've found all kinds of reasons to avoid thinking about your finances.

It's true that the younger you are when you begin to put your financial house in order, the greater the benefits will be as you get older. But it's also true that even if you've put things off for more years than you'd care to think about, it's never too late. Start now.

Take a step-by-step look at the financial decisions you need to make. At the back of this section, you'll find a personal checklist to help you track your progress. You may have already started with some of the basic elements of financial planning or you may want to start at the beginning and work your way through. The important thing is to determine where you are and how you can balance your books and balance your life starting right now.

Four profiles of people that fit this "getting started" kind of financial perspective follow at the end of this section. Check to see if you recognize yourself at certain ages and stages.

What do you really, really want?
So you've told yourself that it's time to get a life. But what kind of life do you want? What are your goals? What are your dreams?

The first step is to identify your goals. They must be clear and measurable so that you can really see the progress you're making. They can be both short term and long term. For example, you may want to reduce your debt, save for a car or a vacation, but down the road you know you'll need funds for your daughter's education and you've always dreamed of retiring in a warm place. All of these dreams can become your reality if you have a plan.

You need to attach a specific dollar amount to each of your short- and long-term goals, so do some research to find out what each one will cost. Then, when you've picked yourself up off the floor, look for ways to find the money. Don't depend on the lottery. Assess your expenses and your spending habits to find places where you can save.

What's your net worth?

My what? Your net worth is a calculation based on what you own, called your assets, and what you owe, your liabilities. It's a snapshot of your financial health. A net worth statement helps to keep you on track and stay focused. So, it's important to review it on a regular basis—perhaps once a year. You'll be surprised how good it feels to see the asset side increase and the liability side decrease and to see that the asset side of your statement is in line with your savings goals. You'll gain a sense of control when you know exactly how much you're worth.

Once you've compiled a net worth statement and can identify where you have to do some work, it's time to set up a budget.

Creating a budget

We've all made the following excuses: I'll start on a budget next month. I can't budget, I don't make enough money. I've tried that but it never works. Budgeting is a very basic element in a financially ordered life. And when you achieve order in one element of life, it's easier to see where you need to rethink some of your other life bloopers. Balance comes from fixing one thing at a time.

Getting it all together

Before you start, you have to want to start. You must decide that budgeting is important to you and that it will take time. So make the time to prepare a budget. And remember that old story. How many psychiatrists does it take to change a lightbulb? None. The lightbulb has to want to change.

- Choose a time when you know you won't be interrupted.
- Choose a place where you're comfortable.
- Gather up all of your monthly bills: rent, utilities, credit cards, gas cards, grocery receipts, dry-cleaning receipts, restaurant stubs, drug store slips, losing lottery tickets.
- Find your pay stub or, if you have automatic pay deposit, get out your bank statement.

I have no idea where the money goes

Your first step will be to complete a Cash In/Outflow worksheet.

- Cash In is your salary and any other income you receive, such as interest, dividends, capital gains, or child support.
- Cash Out is everything you spend: rent/mortgage, insurance, utilities, loan payments, food, clothes, income tax, entertainment, parking, even cat food. Be brutally honest with yourself.
- Total cash inflow minus outflow equals the amount available for your personal goals. The amount could be a surplus or a deficit.
- At this point, many people simply give up and walk away. It may seem too overwhelming to think about your finances, especially if you discover that you have a deficit.

Monitor your spending

Don't give up. Make the time to do this right.

- Get a little notebook and keep it with you at all times (either in your purse or your pocket).
- Each day, write down everything you spend. Do this for one month. Include everything—a newspaper, a bus trip, lunches out, a chocolate bar, a pack of gum, a movie, a bottle of wine.
- One month later, choose a day and time called Budget Day.
- On Budget Day, after you've spent a month tracking everything and every way you spend money, sit down with your Cash In/Outflow

list and the notebook to consolidate your daily tracking of expenses into your Cash In/Outflow.

Now, start the Cash In/Outflow exercise again—but this time pay yourself first.

- Take 10 per cent of your after-tax income and write it in the Cash Out column under "savings."
- List the total of all the things you tracked in your money spent notebook and check to see if all of those items are included in your budget.
- Some things won't change on the Cash Out side, such as your rent, your utilities, or minimum payments.
- However, many other things might change. Take a careful look at your notebook. If you've been really honest with yourself and very careful to make a note of everything, your financial life should be right there in front of you.
- Now the tough part. Deduct the total cash out from the total cash in. If you have a surplus, you'll have to think about a good place to put that extra cash so that you can start earning income on your savings.
- If you have a teeny, tiny surplus or a deficit, you must make some decisions.

Where to cut back?

If you think you can't afford to save, think again. Look at where you might be able to change a few habits and save on the little things that add up to a big total.

- Entertainment?
- Eating out?
- Fast food?
- Too many trips to the clothing store?

Don't make the mistake of cutting out too much, though. You deserve entertainment and clothing allowances. If you make your budget too tough, you'll find it very difficult to stick to your own promises.

It's just like dieting. If you don't choose a sensible plan, you won't be successful and you'll end up overindulging.

Make budgeting easier

Did you know that if you have expenses that throw off your budget on an irregular basis, such as home, auto, life insurance premiums, property taxes or income taxes, you can usually make equal monthly payments? Simply contact the company or the tax office and ask them to arrange monthly payments. Equal monthly payments can make budgeting much easier and it also means no quarterly or annual nasty surprises. Some companies will charge a fee to allow you to pay monthly or quarterly. Find out and then decide whether the extra fee is worth the convenience it provides.

For now, while you're starting to figure out your budget, assume that you are making equal monthly payments. Include in your budget one-twelfth of each annual premium, or one-third of quarterly payments. For example, if you pay $300 every quarter in property taxes, budget $100 per month. If you pay $600 a year in car insurance, list your car insurance monthly payment as $50.

Now that you have a realistic Cash In/Outflow chart, continue tracking your expenses. Keep your little notebook handy and, for another full month, write down everything you buy. One month of tracking your spending will not give you an accurate picture because, without a budget, every month is different. Once you establish a pattern of your spending, you'll never again say, "I have no idea where my money goes."

And here's the real advantage. When you make a habit of tracking every loonie you spend, you become much more conscious of watching your money and you might even think twice about letting the cash fly out of your wallet. Your decision making now makes sense, in the context of a whole plan.

Budgeting tips to avoid overdrafts, plastic, and other black holes
Live within your means. How many times have you heard that?

Now that you have a budget, you know what your "means" means. An honest budget should show you exactly how much disposable income you have. If you go beyond that limit, if you go beyond your means, you'll find yourself in debt. Keep referring back to your Cash In/Outflow worksheet.

Protect your good name
Your credit rating is a measure of how well you've handled your debts. When you borrow money, your name is given to a credit bureau. When you apply for more credit like a bank loan or a credit card or a mortgage, the financial institution contacts the credit bureau to check whether you have paid your debts regularly in the past.

A good credit rating is a really important part of managing your finances. If you've never borrowed money from a financial institution or you don't have a credit card, you won't have a credit rating. And it's really important to have one. To get one, you can apply for a credit card. To keep a good credit rating, make sure you make your payments on time.

Or you could apply for a small loan and pay it back quickly. If you've never borrowed money before, you might have to ask a friend or family member to co-sign the loan. But you'll have to promise your friend that you'll make the payments because co-signing means, if you don't pay, he or she will be on the hook for your debt. This is definitely a bad thing to do to a friend or family member.

Too much debt?
You're on a financial slide down if:

- you spend more than 25 per cent of your take-home pay (not counting your mortgage) to pay off your debts
- you delay paying your regular bills
- you pay only the minimum payment on your credit card balance
- you borrow money to make loan payments

- you have no idea how much you owe
- you have no emergency money

Here are a few tips to help you manage the debt you have and avoid new debt:

- Limit your credit cards. There's no reason to have several credit cards. If you carry only one major credit card, you'll receive one bill and that helps with your budgeting. You'll pay far less interest on one outstanding balance than if you have several cards with several different balances. After all, an outstanding balance has a ticking interest meter attached to it. Every day your balance remains unpaid after the grace period, you pay for it.
- Pay the most expensive debt first—not the one with the highest balance, but the one with the highest interest rate. For example, you should pay down your credit card before your mortgage.
- Don't stop making payments to any creditor. Any interruption of your payment schedule will reflect badly on your credit history.
- Don't try to rank your creditors to determine which one would be the nicest and let you off the hook. You are responsible for paying all of your debts on time.
- If you receive a bonus at work, a tax refund, or a cash gift, think about putting that little windfall directly toward your credit card balance. The sooner you pay off the balance, the more money you'll save in interest charges.
- Perhaps you have a little money hidden away for a rainy day, under your mattress, in a piggy bank, in a savings account. You're thinking, "That's my savings, I can't touch it." Think about this. What interest rate are you earning on your investment? What interest rate are you paying on your credit card debt? It's likely that you're paying more for the debt than you're earning on the savings. If that's true, it's wiser to use the cash to pay down the credit card.
- Make a fresh start. If you find that your budget just won't work for you because you can't get out from under your debts, consider

arranging for a "consolidation loan." What's that? Let's say that you have three credit cards with amounts owing on each, as well as a department-store card and a gas card. And don't forget the money you owe your brother. A consolidation loan is an arrangement to borrow enough money to pay off all of your debts, leaving you with one monthly payment to the lender. That can be preferable to paying a number of debts with scary interest rates. And one monthly payment simplifies budgeting.

Saving feels good—pay yourself first

If the first item on your Cash Outflow column is 10 per cent of your after-tax income for savings, you've already made the commitment to save. Figure out what 10 per cent of your income comes to, then look at your other pre-budget Cash Out items. You'll be surprised to find that if you ignore that money, if you don't even think about it, you really won't miss it with a well-structured budget.

Here's an incentive to ensure that you pay yourself first. Let's say you're 22 years old and you put $100 a month into saving for your retirement from age 22 until age 31 and then stop. Let's assume that your investment pays an average annual return of 8 per cent. Your total investment is $10,800.

If you leave your investment alone, by the time you're 65 and ready to retire, that little bit of savings will have grown to $238,400.

If you're 31 now, the amount will be less but still very significant. Here are the numbers. If you save $100 a month, at 8 per cent annual average return, from now until you're 65, you'll have $212,400.

But, since you started later, your total investment would have been $40,800—a whole lot more than the $10,800 in the earlier example.

So don't put it off any longer. Start today.

I need money right now!

If you don't have insurance and something happens to your stuff, what would you do? Or what if your car needs major repairs and you're living from pay cheque to pay cheque? What if your aunt dies in British

Columbia and you live in the Maritimes and you have to attend the funeral tomorrow? What if your company decided to downsize your position?

An emergency fund is something everyone should have. It's really a savings fund that you might have to use. Think of it as your own little insurance policy.

Your emergency fund should equal three to six months' expenses. Although that may seem like a lot, think how important it is and start now to save a little every pay period. (Don't forget to include your savings in your monthly budget.) Until your fund builds up, think about what else you might do. You can, if you absolutely have to, cash in your RRSPs. You may hate doing that because you know your investment won't build if it's not there and the funds are taxable when you withdraw them. The good news, however, is that if you're cashing in your RRSP because you're unemployed, it is likely that the income level at which you'll be taxed will be low.

Another option that you can arrange immediately is a personal line of credit. This is a loan that you arrange to use when you need it. If you don't need the funds and don't use the funds, you won't be charged any interest. But, just like plastic, if you use up your line of credit, you won't have it when you really need it. You know what to tell yourself: "This is real money, this is real money."

Piggy Banks, Mattresses, and Even Smarter Ways to Save

Stashing your cash in a piggy bank, cookie jar, or under the mattress may be some good old-fashioned ways to save but the concept is a bit flawed. If you can get your hands on your money quickly and easily then you're not really saving—you're simply delaying spending. What's really important is to find a way to save that makes your money work for you.

Nobody said saving was easy, particularly if you have a few spending genes in your system. Because it's difficult, we must play little tricks on ourselves to force us to accept the idea that some money is not meant to be spent.

Direct withdrawal savings

One of the easiest ways to save is through automatic withdrawals from your account into savings. That means every week or every month a predetermined amount will be withdrawn from your account and placed in a savings plan.

Your banker can help you decide what's best. She'll help you develop a personal savings profile by asking you a number of questions. How you save will depend on your personal goals.

Then it's up to you to decide how much you want to save. Your money will be automatically withdrawn from your account every month or every week. You can arrange the withdrawal to coincide with your pay day. Soon you won't even think about it anymore and when your savings are part of a sensible budget, you won't even miss the money.

Start saving

There are some basic facts about saving that you probably already know but bankers and accountants have their own language. So listen up.

- The power of time is a life maxim applied to money—you know, "time marches on"; "sands through the hourglass"; "too soon old, too late smart." The sooner you start saving, the better off you'll be. There are two reasons for this. The first is obvious: if you save for five years, you'll have more than if you save for one. The second element of the power of time is compounding. That's earning income on your income. In other words, your savings produce income so your savings grow. The income on the savings grows too, making more savings. Trust me. Start saving now.

RRSPs—What are they?

Registered Retirement Savings Plans (RRSPs) were introduced by the federal government in 1957, to help Canadians save for their retirement. So, they're for older people? Wrong. RRSPs are for everyone who works and plans to retire eventually. Even if retirement is the last thing on your mind, you can benefit from saving in an RRSP.

What's in my RRSP?

An RRSP is an umbrella that covers, or a basket that contains, a whole range of investments. There are many kinds of products, including mutual funds. These investments differ according to the risk you're willing to take, the time you plan to continue to save, and the amount of income you need. Your banker or financial planner can help you match your financial objectives, your risk, and investor profile to the choice of investments.

Some of the eligible investments for an RRSP include:

- bonds
- T-bills
- stocks
- mutual funds
- GICs

You can choose which of these products will make up your RRSP or, like most people, you can let your financial planner help you choose the products. To get started, you simply have to tell your advisor, "I'd like to open an RRSP."

Why would I?

Here are a few very good reasons to open an RRSP:

- All contributions to an RRSP are currently deductible, within certain limits. That means you not only save but you'll pay less income tax now.

- The money you save grows faster because what you earn on the investment in your RRSP is also tax-deferred until it is cashed.
- When you retire and withdraw your RRSP savings, you'll have to pay tax, but it is likely that by that time, your income level will be lower. The tax rate at that time will therefore likely be lower than the tax rate at which you're saving now.

Does everyone need insurance?

What is life insurance? We mortals don't like to talk about death. We pretend we're immortal. It's easier that way. Unfortunately, there's no one around to prove that's true.

Life insurance can be a very practical financial investment for people who know they are mortal. In fact, the concept was invented when mortality was part of the job. Hundreds of years ago, many ships set sail from England to exotic places all over the world, but many did not return. Not the goods nor the sailors. Insurance was invented to protect both the cargo and the crew in the event of a shipwreck. A possibly doomed sailor could set out knowing that if he did not return, his wife and children would not be left destitute.

Bad planners said, "I'll pay you back when my ship comes in." Smart planners knew they could meet their obligations, ship, or no ship. Few of us sail for a living anymore but none of us live forever. That's why everyone should at least think about life insurance.

- Life insurance pays a fixed amount of money to a named beneficiary of the insured person who has died. (The beneficiary is the person who benefits from the insurance money.)
- Life insurance is purchased by paying a monthly or annual payment, called a premium, to the insurer.
- You can purchase life insurance:
  –to provide money to your relatives or friends after your death
  –to cover the cost of your funeral
  –to pay off your debts after you die
  –to be able to provide an income for a partner or children

–to ensure that the mortgage is paid and your family can continue to live in their home

–as a savings vehicle for education or retirement, or

–as a way to make a charitable donation upon your death by designating the charity as the beneficiary

Why should you buy insurance?

The first reason to buy insurance is to acknowledge that you're mortal. It's amazing how facing life's greatest inevitability puts you on the road to thinking about your life in a more balanced way.

There are many different kinds of insurance, with a wide range of amounts payable to obtain the differing benefits provided by the various products. And, of course, the amount and type of insurance you'll need will depend on the reasons you're purchasing it. For instance, if you want insurance for your funeral, the death benefit amount needed would be quite modest. But, if you're planning to leave a considerable inheritance to your family, you would have to purchase a policy that provides a much larger death benefit amount.

Term insurance

Term insurance is what it says it is—life insurance for a certain number of years, a specified time, or term. Term insurance pays out an agreed-upon amount of money called the face value or death benefit to the beneficiary named in the policy at the time of death of the insured person.

The insured might want to purchase insurance on her life for 5, 10, or 20 years. Some people decide on term insurance because they recognize the need for insurance protection, particularly if they have a small amount of savings. As they get older and have built up their savings, the need for an emergency lump sum of money may be less urgent.

When the term on the insurance policy is over, the policy expires. Many term insurance policies can be renewed for another term but with some companies you may have to re-qualify for the insurance, at which time the rates are often higher. As you get older, the cost of term insurance gets higher and the ability to renew may terminate at a specific age.

There is a plan called "Term to 100," which means the insurance will stay in effect until age 100. There is no need to renew this type of term insurance and the amount you pay for it remains the same for the whole term.

There is no build-up of cash value in a term policy. It is insurance coverage providing a death benefit only. For that reason, term insurance is the least expensive life insurance product available.

Permanent insurance

Permanent or "whole life" insurance has more benefits than term insurance, including a savings component that grows over a certain period of time. Since permanent insurance builds up a cash value, it is more expensive to purchase. The savings that build up in your whole life policy are not taxable, except when they exceed the cost of providing mortality insurance.

Universal life

Many companies offer insurance that is a blend of term and permanent insurance. That means you can have the benefit of a savings portion of your policy (which may be taxable), without paying the often expensive premiums on permanent insurance. Universal life combines the protection coverage of term insurance and the savings part of permanent insurance. Today's universal life policies allow you to choose how your policy's savings are invested. With an array of investments ranging from GICs and bonds to equities, you have the opportunity to determine the risk/return for your policy. As well, investment growth is not taxed within the policy, and will flow tax-free to your beneficiary as a death benefit.

When should I buy life insurance?

Here's a big mistake: "I'll buy life insurance when I'm older. I don't need it now." The rates you pay for your insurance premium are determined by your age and state of health. The younger and healthier you are, the less expensive your premiums will be. If the cost of permanent insurance seems too high for you now, you might consider purchasing term insurance and then converting to permanent insurance later.

If you can agree that at some time in your life you will need life insurance, then now is the time to buy it, when you're young and healthy.

Gambling with fate is a sure sign of an unbalanced life. Life can be long and full and rich, particularly when you make realistic plans and wise decisions. And the bonus is you'll not only feel proud of yourself for being practical, but you'll also have purchased a little peace of mind.

Group insurance

Many companies and associations offer group life insurance to their employees or members. Some companies pay the premiums on your insurance, while others offer the opportunity to join the plan and pay your own premiums. Usually the premiums are at lower rates than you would pay if you were buying insurance directly. Check it out:

- Find out whether your company offers a group insurance plan.
- Check whether you have to pay the premiums and if so, how much.
- You might want to check around to determine whether buying insurance on your own might be a better choice for you, particularly if you're young and healthy.
- And remember, if you have group insurance through a company plan, you are covered under the plan only as long as you are employed with the company.

Disability insurance

It's a zoo out there and sometimes, when you least expect it, that old banana peel is under your foot and your feet slide out from under you. Ouch.

A disability that prevents you from earning a living is another one of life's nasty realities. And another reason to prepare yourself for what might happen. The chances aren't really that remote. If you're 30, the odds are three to one that you'll be disabled at some time before you die. By 50, the odds are two to one. Why gamble?

Your employer may provide disability coverage as part of a group benefits plan but not all companies do, so make sure you check it out. You have to determine how much your plan covers and for how long. Don't forget that your plan will no longer be in place when you stop working for that employer. And don't assume that the government will take care of you. Government plans are there but, for most people, the benefits are nowhere near the income they'll eventually need.

If you're self-employed, the only person you can count on to earn a living is you. That's why, unless you want to live dangerously and play the odds, you must have disability insurance.

How does it work?
Disability insurance normally pays 66 ⅔ per cent of your income, at the time of disability. Plans vary from company to company. When you choose a plan, you'll have to determine:

- your monthly expenses
- how long you'll need disability income
- how long your savings would last, if you needed to use them
- the effect on your retirement savings
- other sources of income

There are numerous disability plans and many companies offering them. Compare:

- the cost
- the benefits
- how long you'll receive the benefits
- how long you have to wait before the benefits kick in
- the rules specifying the nature of the job your disability must prevent you from performing in order to qualify for benefit payments

Protect your stuff

We have a lot invested in our "stuff." Whether you have a big house with lots of furniture and china and paintings or whether you have a bachelor apartment with a couch, a television, and a VCR, your stuff needs protection. That's why it's really important to protect your valuables from fire, flood, and theft.

If you have a home, you must have home insurance to qualify for a mortgage. The lender wants to ensure that in case your home is damaged in a fire, you'll have enough money to get it fixed or to rebuild. The lending institution wants to protect its investment, which makes sense.

But what about your stuff?

When you buy home insurance, you'll be asked about the value of the contents of your home. The insurer will insure your home for an amount sufficient to cover the cost of fixing or replacing your home as well as its contents. You'll have to think about what you have and determine a price that you believe represents the value of your furniture, clothes, jewellery, appliances, tools, books, artwork, and knick-knacks.

And, of course, you need to think about owners' liability coverage, in case the newspaper delivery girl slips on your snow-covered steps.

If you rent, you don't need insurance on the actual building because the building's owner will already have insurance on it. But if your valuables are lost in a fire, you may not ever see enough money to replace them. And if someone breaks in and steals your treasures, you're out of luck. If you have anything of value that you can't afford to replace (in the event of a fire, flood, or theft), contact a general insurance agent or broker. Some insurance agents or brokerages sell both life insurance and general insurance. Others sell only one or the other. And, of course, you still need to consider liability coverage.

The premiums for home and contents insurance are very reasonable considering the value of your possessions. You may be surprised to discover how little it costs to protect your stuff.

Auto insurance

If you own or lease a car, you must have auto insurance to drive it anywhere. You can't license your car until you have insurance.

The amount you pay for your auto insurance will depend on a few factors, such as your age, your driving record (parking tickets not included), and the make, model, and year of your car. For instance, if you've had three speeding tickets and an accident and you want to buy a new Corvette, you will pay a big premium for your insurance. In other words, your driving record and taste for fast cars raise the possibility that you might have an accident and make a claim.

On the other hand, if you've never had a ticket or an accident and you want to buy a mid-size economy car, your premiums will be lower. Rates vary from province to province and from one insurance company or broker to another. In fact, some provinces insist that car insurance be purchased through a provincial authority. In any event, it's essential to do your homework and ensure that you receive the best deal and the best service.

Where do I buy home and auto insurance?

If you're looking for home or auto insurance, ask family members, friends, co-workers, or neighbours for referrals. Everyone you know who has a home or a car has made an insurance decision. Take the names of a few people and companies and shop around for a good price. Some companies today offer quotes (suggested prices) over the phone and via the Internet. And don't forget to add the premium costs to your monthly budget!

Your First Home

What a big decision. You're planning to buy a house? Congratulations! But where do you start?

Because it is a big decision and a big purchase, you have good reason to feel nervous. But there is a step-by-step way to determine what you can afford and to find out all the information you'll need to make the right decision. Before you know it, you'll be planting your first tree in your backyard.

Can I afford it?

Well, let's find out.

Lenders, including financial institutions, have developed a formula to help people to determine whether they can afford to buy a home. Lenders have adopted this approach because some people want a house so badly they think they can make some sacrifices and cut back on other things. What they often discover, however, is that they have a house but they can't afford to buy furniture or to pay the plumber when the sink is dripping.

Most lenders agree that you shouldn't spend more on your house than 30 to 32 per cent of your gross monthly income (gross is the amount on your pay cheque before deductions or taxes). That amount of your salary must cover the cost of mortgage payments, property taxes, and utilities (heat and water).

Before you go house hunting, however, there's another consideration. The lender will want to know about your total "debt service ratio," which refers to everything you owe: the costs associated with the house you want to buy plus your existing debts, such as credit cards.

For these reasons, it's a good idea to visit your lender before you start house hunting to determine how much you can afford. If you have an acceptable debt service ratio and credit, your lender can arrange a pre-approved mortgage that fits with what you can afford.

A pre-approved mortgage is useful because once you've found the house you like, you can make a conditional offer and then contact the lender to say that you're ready to finalize the mortgage.

Now you can start looking at houses. But what kind? Here's a simple way to determine what kind of house you can afford. Multiply your annual income by 2.5. For instance, if you make $40,000 a year, you can afford to buy a house that costs roughly $100,000, as long as any of your other debts are not too high. But, your lender can only lend you part of the purchase price of the house. You also need a down payment.

No down payment?

Do you have a savings plan? Are you paying yourself first?

If buying a home is one of your goals, then you've already thought about how much you'll need to save and how much time it will take.

You might want to check out the federal government's Home Buyers' Plan. Here's a brief summary of how it works.

If you qualify, you may withdraw up to $20,000 from your RRSP to use as a down payment on your house. If you and your partner plan to own the home together, then both of you can withdraw $20,000 from your RRSP. That means, as a couple, you can withdraw $40,000. Usually when you withdraw money from your RRSP, you must pay income tax on the amount withdrawn. But with the Home Buyers' Plan, you don't have to pay that tax as long as you pay back the amount you withdrew from your RRSP, in equal minimum instalments, within 16 years.

This plan used to be for first-time homeowners only. But since 1998, the plan changed to allow you to participate again, as long as you've repaid the funds from the first time you participated, and as long as you haven't owned a home in the last five years.

For more information on the Home Buyers' Plan, contact your financial planner or the General Enquiries section of your tax services office.

Is it realistic for you?

Before choosing to participate in the Home Buyers' Plan, carefully consider the following points:

- When you pay back the money to your RRSP, there's no tax deduction.
- Can you afford to pay it back, knowing that this time there'll be no tax deduction?
- If you don't pay back your minimum payment one year, the shortfall is added to your earned income on your tax return, and you will be taxed on this amount.
- When you use your RRSP savings, you lose the compound growth.
- Weigh your decision carefully, against the quality of life, security, and potential return on investment that comes from home ownership.

If owning a home is one of your dreams, start today and make it happen.

Mortgage language you'll need to learn

Now that you have your down payment, you'll need to arrange for the rest of the financing for your home through a mortgage. There are two basic types of mortgages, depending on the amount of your down payment:

- You can get a conventional mortgage if you have 25 per cent of the cost of the house as a down payment, of which 15 per cent must be from your own resources. For example, on a house that was appraised at and purchased for $100,000, the lender will lend you $75,000 if you have $25,000 in cash to make a down payment.
- You may borrow up to 75 per cent of the appraised value or the purchase price, whichever is lower.
- If you don't have a 25 per cent down payment, you may want to apply for a high-ratio mortgage. This kind of mortgage allows you to buy a home even if you have only 5 per cent as a down payment. Your mortgage will have to be approved by the Canada Mortgage and Housing Corporation (CMHC) or GE Capital. An insurance premium is also applied.
- The term of your mortgage can be anywhere from six months to ten years. When interest rates are high, it's often a good idea to agree to a shorter-term mortgage so you can change your contract when interest rates go down, and save money on your payments.
- Interest rates can vary. The rates depend on the state of the economy and the rates set by various lenders. It's very important to determine the amount you can afford since the interest rate is fixed for the term of your mortgage. Some people decide to delay their home-buying decision when rates are particularly high.
- The amortization period is the amount of time it will take to pay off your mortgage completely; that is, the time you will have a mortgage on your home. A standard amortization period is 25 years.
- Renewal. When the term of your mortgage ends, your mortgage comes up for renewal. At that time, interest rates may have changed

or your income may have changed. At renewal time you can change your amortization period to a shorter period or you can renew, based on the original amortization period. That decision will depend on whether you want to pay the same monthly payment or perhaps a little more or a little less.

- PIT. Your mortgage payment is made up of Principal (the amount that goes against what you borrowed) and Interest (the cost of borrowing the mortgage money). But you'll also have to pay property taxes on your home. You can choose to pay those yourself, usually in quarterly payments, or you can ask your lender to blend your property taxes into your payment. This is a good idea for people on a budget. When you pay principal, interest, and taxes (PIT), you don't have to worry about saving for your quarterly tax payments.

- Weekly, biweekly, or monthly payments. Whichever option you choose, the more frequently you make a payment, the sooner you'll pay down your mortgage. For example, if your mortgage is $150,000 and your monthly payment is $1050, at a rate of 7 per cent you'll pay $165,170 in interest over 25 years, when your mortgage is finally paid off. On the other hand, if you pay $525.00 biweekly, your mortgage will be paid off in 20.5 years and you'll have paid $129,350 in interest. What a difference!

Most lenders allow you to double up on your payments and pre-pay up to 10 per cent of the original principal of the mortgage once each calendar year.

Other costs you should know about

When you purchase a home, you'll have to pay a number of costs. You'll need a lawyer to handle the transaction. You'll need to make sure you have homeowner's insurance and there may be applicable land taxes.

Your real estate agent, lawyer, or lender can help you determine just how much these costs may be. Make sure to consider all of these costs.

Buying a home is a big decision. But it doesn't have to be just a dream. If you really want something in your life, you plan for it, save for it, and decide you can do it.

Happy house-hunting!

Whatever your dream, you can make it work for you. A road is never long if it's measured step by step. That's what getting started is all about. It means taking charge, turning red ink to black, and focusing on what you really want. Few people are handed health, wealth, and happiness. Most choose to have it and choose to work for it. You can too.

Financial Health Check-up

To summarize how you're doing so far, keep the following checklist in mind as you measure your progress in getting closer to more balanced financial health.

THE "GETTING STARTED" CHECKLIST

                                                                Completion date

- I have a financial plan that includes what I want and how I'm getting there.   _____
- I have a budget that's realistic for me.   _____
- I always stick to my budget.   _____
- I know what my credit rating is.   _____
- My debt is under control.   _____
- I have a savings plan that I contribute to regularly.   _____
- I have an emergency fund.   _____
- I contribute to an RRSP.   _____
- I have a plan to buy a house.   _____
- I have life insurance.   _____
- I have auto insurance.   _____
- I have home insurance.   _____
- I have disability insurance.   _____

Personal Perspectives on the Challenges of Achieving a Richer, More Fulfilling Lifestyle

As you meet the following individuals and understand their personal situations, you may see something of yourself at a certain age or stage of your life.

Following each woman's story are constructive suggestions on how she might deal with the challenges she's facing today. Some of these pointers might also relate to you and your ability to enhance your chance to achieve greater balance and personal fulfillment.

Barbara

Age: 57 (widowed/two grown children)
Occupation: Part-time secretary

FINANCIAL SNAPSHOT

Assets		Liabilities	
House	$200,000	Mortgage	$150,000
Car	$4,500		
RRSPs	$9,000		
Total Assets:	$213,500	Total Liabilities:	$150,000

Estimated Net Worth: $63,500

Estimated Cash Flow
Net Monthly Income $2,100

Key Monthly Expenses
Investment Programs $nil
Household Expenses $550
Mortgage/Rent $1,300
Insurance Plans $65

Monthly Expenses (cont'd)

Debt Payments	$nil
Discretionary Expenses	$150
Total Income	$2,100
Total Expenses	$2,065

Personal snapshot

"When can I retire? This is what I want to know. My husband passed away recently after a lengthy illness, and our savings were exhausted by the expenses of long-term homecare. Frank had run a small corner store for all his life. We made a living at it, but of course he didn't have a pension, and he couldn't keep up with his life insurance payments so we lost that. As a part-time worker, I have no company pension and will have to rely on the government in retirement.

"Frank used to say our one asset was our house. We bought it during the recession, it's in a good neighbourhood, and before Frank got ill, it had appreciated enough for him to be able to get a $150,000 mortgage. He needed it for the business. He was trying to expand. Now, I feel it's my one asset. I don't want to sell because Frank and I put so much in the house and garden. On the other hand, I might have a better time if I didn't have to pay a mortgage, and had some cash on hand.

"My children are grown and they're great. Neal's a doctor just starting out. He's paying off student loans and trying to raise a family. Clare's married too but she lives far away. I don't see either of them very often, I rely much more on friends. And I have lots of good ones. I was a runner in high school and I still like to jog. But you know, my greatest pleasure is my regular book club meetings. Frank and I once loved to read aloud to each other and go to the theatre. I'd love to live like that again. Recently, the real estate agent told me that the market was getting hotter. I'm tempted. Is it time to start over?"

FQ rating: C

Considerations: The loss of your significant other after a ten-year illness takes a long time to work through. Being widowed is one of those critical, enormously difficult passages of life. And as so often happens, your children are not in a position to help you financially. This is much more common than you would think. You've been part of a unit. On your own, the world looks different and often more unfriendly than it actually is. I think it's great you have a book club.

The upside is that you have skills that many young people don't often have! A skilled and reliable secretary is always employable. The question of when you can retire will depend on what you choose to do with respect to your house and if you want to use it as a source of income. This is where you have to determine what you really want and what your expectations are for the future.

You do have options and exploring them will help you to make decisions. To explore the option of selling your house you may want to get it appraised by a couple of agents and get some opinions from them on the chances of selling it well. You might also ask them what their sales strategy would be. Sometimes if it's a hot market, an agent will ask for bids to be made within say, five days. In a hot market, you may be able to get more for your house than you otherwise would.

If this is a bad time to sell, how about investigating the future of your neighbourhood? Is it becoming attractive to developers? If so, perhaps you should keep the house and explore your other options. What about taking in a lodger? Your house sounds large enough for you to do so and keep your privacy. I realize that a grown child living with Mom can be a trial, but if Neal is having trouble paying off his student loans, perhaps he and his family could move in with you and share expenses.

Carol

Age:	44 (divorced/re-married)
Occupation:	Paramedic

FINANCIAL SNAPSHOT

Assets		Liabilities	
House	$160,000	Mortgage	$36,000
Car	$8,000	Credit Card Debt	$1,340
Savings	$5,000		

Assets (cont'd)

RRSPs	$4,000
Stocks	$5,000

Total Assets:	$182,000	Total Liabilities:	$37,340

Estimated
  Net Worth: $144,660

Estimated Cash Flow
Net Monthly Income $2,500

Monthly Expenses

Investment Programs	$nil
Household Expenses	$600
Mortgage/Rent	$640
Insurance Plans	$60
Debt Payments	$65
Discretionary Expenses	$250

Total Income	$2,500
Total Expenses	$1,615

Personal snapshot

"Five years ago, I went through a mid-life crisis. Today, I feel on top of the world. Back at that time, I gave up my life-long career as an actress and my marriage fell apart. Today, I have a great new job and a great new husband.

"At first, it wasn't easy. I literally woke up one morning and decided I could no longer hack it as an actress in regional theatre. I was getting older and the opportunities were fewer, and I was tired of selling myself all the time. I should have gone south 20 years before. Now I was surviving on bit parts in American movies in Vancouver. On top of that, my husband and I split up. It had been coming for some time. But all of a sudden, my life collapsed.

"My first panic was where would I live? I shared my house with my first husband, but he let me buy him out. Actually the bank loaned me the money. That was my first lifesaver. Then my therapist advised me to go to a job counsellor. What did I see myself doing? Something physical, I found myself saying.

"At the Health Club, I heard about paramedics. I took a year's course, there were only 10 women in the class of 60, and I enjoyed the whole experience. I easily passed the weightlifting part of the exam even though I'm only 5 foot 3 inches, and weigh 111 lbs. I have to get up at 4.30 in the mornings just to do push-ups so I'm ready for the first body of the day. When I told my chiropractor what I was going to do, he said 'Great, I'll see more of you.' He's right. I have an appointment every two months and in addition, every month I get a massage. I just can't afford a back injury so I go to the gym three times a week and lift weights regularly. I also take Tai Chi to balance me out and help me relax.

"I met my present husband a year ago. In the ambulance! He was a developer who broke his leg inspecting a new mall construction. On the way to hospital, there was an almighty traffic jam. He was in agony and we couldn't do much for him, so I tried to distract him by singing numbers from old musicals. He laughed so hard that he said I was a cure. He looked me up afterwards and after a very short time, we got married.

"Harry's 10 years older than me, and like me, he's divorced. He's paying big alimony (I have none) and his income goes up and down, so he always seems short. However, he's got life insurance and RRSPs. We've made wills in each others' favour. I am determined to be independent, so I moonlight for extra cash. My acting background got me a job at the medical school: I show actors how to be patients so the students can work with them! This adds almost $10,000 annually to my income. I put as much as I can into my mutual funds. This may change because Harry, who has taken over my investments, wants to see me take more of a flyer with fast-growing high tech or telecommunications or medical technology stocks. I don't know enough about the stock market. His talk makes me nervous.

"My union gives me disability and life insurance and I have a defined pension, 75% of my last five years' salary. My only luxury is the car, but I also need that for my job. We share household expenses. I try to keep to the budget we've agreed on, but Harry loves spontaneity and last-minute surprises.

"My main concern is that I can't put enough into RRSPs. I really worry about the fact that I didn't even have one until I was 38. I don't know how well off I'll be when I retire. Then I worry about whether I'll get to retirement. I may become disabled and have to find other work. I've been investigating the possibility of getting a desk job with the union.

"We live in my house, but Harry is urging me to sell, suggesting that we then buy a bigger house in a better part of town. He had to give his house to his ex-wife, so basically, I would be putting up the capital while he would pay the monthly mortgage. But what would happen if I had to carry the house? He is nearing 60 and I feel we would be overextending ourselves."

FQ rating: C

Considerations: It's quite an achievement to come out of a mid-life crisis and embrace a new life the way you have. Your life is full of pluses, from the new partner, to your financial assets, your pattern of saving, and investments.

Having a new partner enhances your life socially, and it also brings a new player into your finances. Harry's 10 years older than you and that's a very important gap. He's facing retirement fairly soon. You're not. He's also making suggestions about how you use your money—and of course, that's only natural. However, as you say, you aren't very sophisticated about financial matters, and I would like to suggest that you get some expert help. It's not difficult to find it. Today banks can offer such advice. Harry, of course, should be part of this.

A partnership must always be equal and it seems as though you may require a more open and frank discussion about finances with Harry. You obviously have some misgivings at the prospect of moving to "a bigger house in a better part of town" with all the financial responsibilities that would accompany it, to say nothing of Harry's age and impending retirement.

It appears you have some cash left over each month. Why isn't that going into savings and RRSPs? Wouldn't that make you feel better about your financial future? I would like to see you exploring with a financial advisor what your future options may be. For example, you may be eligible for early retirement, which you may like to take in order to spend more time with Harry. What kind of pension will you then get? Have you discovered whether you can get a desk job with the union? Is it possible to work part-time for the union and then find more freelance work? At this point in your life with Harry, it would seem that you need to build in as much flexibility as you can without sacrificing your own financial security.

Cherry

Age: 29 (married/two children)
Occupation: Lab Technician

FINANCIAL SNAPSHOT

Joint Assets		*Liabilities*	
House	$190,000	Mortgage	$150,000
Savings	$1,200	Family Loan	$14,000
Total Assets:	$191,200	Total Liabilities:	$164,000

Estimated Net Worth: $27,200

Estimated Cash Flow
Net Monthly Income $2,000

Cherry's Key Monthly Expenses

Investment Programs	$30
Household Expenses	$640
Mortgage/Rent	$500
Insurance Plans	$20

Monthly Expenses (cont'd)
Debt Payments $600
Discretionary Expenses $200

Total Income $2,000
Total Expenses $1,990

Personal snapshot

"I come from a very traditional culture and I never expected that at 29, I'd have both a family and a job outside the home. I feel very successful with a few reservations.

"My family came to Canada when I was 5. Until I went to college, I knew very little about life outside my family, which is very large and includes aunts and uncles, grandparents, cousins and their wives and husbands. In my family, the women are expected to be wives. My father was unusual because he insisted that my sisters and I go to college.

"At the same time, my big family has helped me with everything. They loaned my father the money so I could go to college, and they loaned me money so I could buy a house.

"Tommy, my husband, and I have a joint bank account but he decides how to spend our money. He's earning good wages at a courier company. I've asked him about whether we should be setting aside money for RRSPs, but he thinks we should put our savings back into the family, the old family way.

"But one of my sisters is an accountant, and she keeps talking about the need to save for retirement, that the Canada Pension Plan may not be here for us when we're old. My parents don't seem to care. The family will somehow provide. Tommy has told me he's taken out life insurance so if anything happens to him, the children and I will have some money. I asked should I do the same but he said 'No.'

"I'd like to improve our house, but Tommy is against borrowing more from the family. My sister said we could get some kind of home improvement loan from the bank, but Tommy doesn't like that idea either. I'd like to buy a car. I could do more with the children and I too could get out more, look up old college friends. At the moment, I just seem to shuttle between home and work."

FQ rating: C

Considerations: Cherry, the financial problems you face are not unique to you, though that likely won't make you feel much better about them. Yet I've met many women in similar circumstances—young women who are trying to combine marriage, family, and a demanding job, and at the same time who are anxious to learn how best to handle the money they earn.

Looking over your financial profile, I wonder whether you might be depriving yourself and your children of things you need in order to repay your family fast. Have you talked to your sisters about your situation? They may be in a similar bind. You may be expecting much more of yourself than your family does.

Have you considered a financial advisor? Your bank can help you there, or perhaps your sisters know a bank advisor who is known in your community.

Once you've given the advisor information about your finances, you might ask specifically about the following. How much should you be saving and putting into RRSPs to ensure a comfortable retirement? Would it be sensible to start a registered education savings plan now for the children's post-secondary education, and if so, what is the best way to go about it? Finally, I would ask about improving the house. Would that be a good investment? Have you found out whether your house has appreciated much since you bought it?

I would bring Tommy into the picture, persuade him if you can to come along with you for a conference at the bank. You're partners and it's important you work toward your goals together. This will require good communication and compromise, but the best partnerships always do. For example, you don't say whether either or both of you have made wills in each others' favour. This is important because children are involved. Also, you might consider taking out life/disability insurance, again with the children's future in mind.

You speak wistfully of your friends from college. Where are they now? With an extremely commendable anxiety to do the best you can for your family, you may have lost sight of your own needs. If a car would give you more freedom, I hope you can get one. Is there any way you can join a family fitness program at a local community centre and take the children along? Do any of your sisters work out regularly? Perhaps you could join them.

Jenny

Age:	23 (single)
Occupation:	Actress/Model

FINANCIAL SNAPSHOT

Assets		*Liabilities*	
Condo	$230,000	Credit Card	$9,000
Car	$15,000	Mortgage	$218,500
Time Share	$15,000		
Savings	$600		
Total Assets:	$260,600	Total Liabilities:	$227,500

Estimated Net Worth: $33,100

Estimated Cash Flow

Net Monthly Income $3,400

Jenny's Key Monthly Expenses

Investment Programs	$100
Household Expenses	$800
Mortgage/Rent	$1,400
Insurance Plans	$120
Debt Payments	$480
Discretionary Expenses	$600
Total Income	$3,400
Total Expenses	$3,500

Personal snapshot

"Last year I earned around $60,000, the year before $6,000! What a difference a zero makes! A pal had got me a gig modelling gloves at a big department store and this guy kept hanging around—and I thought, oh yeah—but then he asked if I'd like to audition for an advertising campaign. Yes! My pal said "Watch it!" But I checked him out and he was okay, and when I saw my first cheque, I flipped. I went right out and bought a car and two weeks in a timeshare that I know I'll need to use as a getaway. Ian, my boyfriend chose it.

"Then Ian says 'Where are we going to live?' I'd seen the pictures of waterfront condos and I had never thought I'd be able to swing one. I had no problem with the 5% downpayment, and they accepted my three-year contract as a guarantee of my income in addition to having a co-signer.

"My Dad told me never to get a credit card, 'You can't handle it, Jen!' He's right, but the moment my face showed up on billboards, I just couldn't resist those credit cards. I went on another spree. I have $9,000 owing. I never thought of repayment. My Dad said 'Ask the bank to help get you on track.'

"So I did. This guy in a suit spent a lot of time getting to know me. He suggested that he make a financial plan for me. He was pleased to see that I have disability insurance from my actors' union, which I had to join when I got my first walk-on in a TV series. He pointed out that despite my three-year contract, in future I still may have irregular pay cheques. I really have to make a budget and stick to it. It's important, he said, to start living within my means. That means paying off my debts. When that's done, he wants to talk to me about mutual funds and an RRSP. I tell you, he opened my eyes a lot. I'm still working it all out.

"I haven't thought of making a will. What's the point? If I made a million overnight, I'd go around the world, get my Mom and Dad a new house, and then give presents to everyone."

FQ rating: C

Considerations: One thing I really like about the Y generation is that you know how to make the best of being young. Your instinct is right: this is not the time to make lifelong commitments. Life's a long time.

I'm not surprised your bank advisor made a point of your living within your means. The most striking aspect of your profile is that you're spending more than you're earning. Instead of using discretionary income, you're using your credit cards for cash flow. If you don't pay credit cards off immediately, the escalating monthly payments can rapidly become an albatross around your neck. And missed payments bump up the interest charges.

Suppose you hit a slump—even though you say your three-year modelling contract is guaranteed—you'd really be struggling to keep up payments. And your lifestyle. Then your credit rating would be damaged and one bad thing would lead to another. Many young people I've met don't really understand how a bad credit rating can hurt their chances of borrowing money at the best rates. You're never too young to lay the groundwork for your life's financial plan.

I'd like to suggest that you keep that $600 in your savings as your emergency fund, and continue saving that amount and just put it toward debt repayment instead. In fact, I'd be inclined to cut my budget in order to pay down the credit cards or you might even consider selling your timeshare. You might find a debt holiday is even more satisfying than a week off. I'm glad to hear you've got a financial advisor at your bank, and I hope you do listen to him. May I suggest something else? You may want to consider sharing household expenses with Ian. This won't compromise your independence and the money may help to reduce your debt even further. Lastly, once you pay off your debt, you might want to think about saving money in an RRSP. Income tax savings could then be applied to your mortgage. This is how to make your net worth grow. Start by determining what is really important to you, and then pay yourself first. You will be surprised how quickly your dreams can become a reality when you're focused.

4 Learn More and Earn More

Financial Tips for Take-charge Women

So, you must feel pretty good about yourself. You scored between 21 and 39 on the quiz.

Assuming that you didn't fudge the numbers, you're well on your way to having a financially balanced life. But like any other element in a well-balanced life, your financial knowledge should continue to grow and become more sophisticated. It's particularly important to monitor your financial plans and do a lot of "re's," like re-planning, re-budgeting, re-investing, and re-jigging before you re-tire.

Maybe that's many, many years down the road. Perhaps it's sooner than you'd care to think about. But you have to think about it. So read on and learn more. You're already doing a pretty good job of taking care of your financial health. Let's see if you can't improve further.

You're feeling some stability in your life and beginning to think more about where you want to be in the next 10 to 20 years. Perhaps you've married, begun to have children, and now you're considering building an investment portfolio. Or you've decided it's time to start building on your investment in yourself.

What if you're not quite where you want to be or thought you were? Don't worry. Go back a few pages and review the checklist at the end of the "Getting Started" section and consider the steps you should be taking now.

After you've read through this section, check the example profiles of women who scored about the same as you did on the quiz. You may see a similarity between them and you, at some age or stage in your life. See whether you can determine what advice you would have given them.

Let's get started.

Everybody's Talkin' about "The Market"

If you're part of the market, you're either a borrower or a lender, because in the big picture there are two types of investments: debt securities and equity securities.

Debt securities

If you invest in a debt security, you're a lender. That means you buy an investment that pays interest. Here's how it works. When governments and companies need to raise money, they issue a debt security, such as a Treasury Bill (T-Bill), or a government or corporate bond.

When you invest, you're making a loan to the government or corporation. The organization then uses your money with the promise that you'll get back what you paid (the principal) after a certain period when your investment matures. And they also promise to pay you a certain amount of interest.

Equity securities

If you invest in an equity security, you're an owner. Your investment has the potential to generate earnings or profits. Companies may issue both debt and equity securities to raise money. Equity means ownership and each share of the company represents part ownership.

When you have stock in a company, you're planning on sharing in the company's success through dividends and increased share prices. There are no guarantees that you'll earn an income or receive a higher price when you sell. But few investments offer greater potential for growth than stocks.

To market, to market

It's always meant the same thing. A market is a place where buyers and sellers meet to carry on commerce and execute transactions. Vegetable markets sell vegetables. Financial markets sell a range of financial investments.

Money market

Money markets are for investors who want to earn competitive rates on their money. Governments and companies go to money markets to borrow. Investments that are bought and sold include short-term debt securities, which usually mature in 18 months or less. Some investments can include government Treasury Bills, bankers' acceptances, and commercial paper.

Fixed-income market

Investors typically leave their money in this market for a longer period, from one to 30 years. Governments and companies come to a fixed-income market when they need money for a longer term. Investments bought and sold in this market include government and corporate bonds, and mortgage-backed securities.

Equity (stock) market

These are the more well-known markets where stocks are bought and sold. Some are "real" (The New York Stock Exchange—NYSE). Others are now fully electronic, so you won't see any floor traders dealing in strange sign language, such as on the NASDAQ in New York and, recently, the Toronto Stock Exchange (TSE).

Markets have class

Investments traded in the money market, fixed income, and equity markets fall into three "asset classes": safety, income, and growth.

- Safety usually relates to preserving your original investment, consisting of investments that offer moderately low risk and moderately low returns.

- Income usually corresponds to investments that provide a higher level of income with relatively low risk but higher risk and higher potential returns than safety investments.
- Growth or equity-oriented investments usually present higher risk with the highest potential return.

Which investment is right for me?

Once again, your banker or financial planner can direct you to the types of investments that are most appropriate for you, given your age, your goals, the kind of risks you are willing to take, and your time horizon.

The risk/return trade-off is a rule that is often discussed. Each asset class has a different level of risk and anticipated return. The higher the risk, the greater the chance of significant growth. But risk is risk and you might not see the growth you hoped for in the time frame you expected and, in fact, you may experience a loss on your investment.

The lower the risk, the lower the potential return on your savings. That's the trade-off. For those who believe that "slow and steady wins the race," low-risk investments are a good thing in a well-balanced portfolio.

Safety first

Safety investments should be included as part of a well-balanced portfolio. These investments provide stability and liquidity, and help reduce overall risk. And they're great for building an emergency fund or saving for a short-term goal. Most safety investments are considered RRSP-eligible.

Safety investments are considered the same as cash because you can usually cash them in quickly (they're "liquid") and there's little chance that you'll lose on your capital investment. Safety-class investments include bank accounts, short-term GICs, term deposits, and money market mutual funds.

Earn an income

Fixed-income investments are another part of a well-balanced portfolio. They provide a regular stream of income to supplement your salary or your pension or your savings. And they have the potential to generate capital gains whenever interest rates go down (or capital losses when interest rates move higher).

Fixed-income investments include government bonds (which are considered the safest Canadian fixed-income investment), provincial and municipal bonds, mortgage-backed securities, and fixed-income mutual funds.

Watch 'em grow

Growth investments are also part of a well-balanced portfolio because they provide the potential for higher returns. Growth potential helps you build toward your goals more quickly and protects your portfolio against a loss of purchasing power resulting from inflation. But don't overlook the risk: they also experience more ups and downs along the way.

When you're investing in growth, you're participating in the performance of publicly traded companies listed on the stock exchange. Their success can be your success.

Home of the bulls and the bears

Stocks are bought and sold at stock exchanges, which can be a real location or an electronic market. They are private organizations composed of companies called member firms. The performance of the market is measured by indices. An index is a broad representation of a market and is considered the benchmark for performance of that market. There are several in the North American market, including the TSE 300 Composite Index, Dow Jones Industrial Average, and S&P 500 Stock Price Index.

- The Toronto Stock Exchange (TSE 300 Composite Index) is the major index for the Canadian stock market. It comprises 300 representative Canadian companies listed on the TSE.
- The Dow Jones Industrial Average is the most famous index in the world. It's based on a weighted-average of 30 industrials that trade on the New York Stock Exchange (NYSE).
- Standard & Poor's (S&P) 500 Stock Price Index is made up of 400

industrial stocks and 100 utility, financial, and transportation stocks, most of which trade on the NYSE.

Mutual funds—what are they?

Everyone into the pool! That's what mutual funds are—pools of money made up of a lot of people's investments. Professional managers invest this money in a broad portfolio of investments according to specific objectives. Your mutual fund manager is an expert at putting money in different investments, trying to get the best rate of return possible within the stated objective of the mutual fund.

Where are they?

Everywhere. You can purchase a mutual fund through your bank, trust company, financial planner, stockbroker, insurance company, or a mutual fund company.

Why would I invest in mutual funds?

CONVENIENCE

Buying and selling mutual funds can be as easy as speaking with a registered mutual fund representative at your local bank branch, or contacting your financial planner or broker or contacting the company directly, even on the Internet. Regular account statements and reports simplify your record keeping.

PROFESSIONAL MANAGEMENT

Some people don't have the time, resources, or experience to stay abreast of financial trends and evaluate individual stocks and bonds. Professional money managers make the investment decisions for all mutual fund holders.

AFFORDABILITY

Depending on the mutual fund, minimum investments can be as low as $25 per fund if you make regular purchases through a pre-authorized purchase plan. The amount you select is transferred directly from your bank account at regular intervals—weekly, monthly, or on payday—and invested in your mutual fund.

FLEXIBILITY

If your fund is part of a group or "family" of funds, you can often move some or all of your money from one fund to another within the group or family as your needs change or new opportunities arise.

DIVERSIFICATION

A basic principle of sound investing is to spread your portfolio over a range of investments. This risk-reduction technique reduces the impact that one poor choice can have on your overall portfolio. Mutual funds can hold any number of different securities, with some holding from 50 to 100 different securities. Most investors would find it difficult and expensive to assemble a portfolio of that size on their own.

RRSP-ELIGIBILITY

Mutual funds are an excellent way to take advantage of the benefits of tax-sheltered investing through RRSPs. Most Canadian funds are 100 per cent RRSP-eligible, while most global funds are eligible for the 20 per cent foreign-content limit.

Risky Business?

Many people are afraid to invest in things they don't understand. And that's a good sign. But if you're just starting out, you don't need to know all the in and outs, all the different types of funds, all the levels of investment risks—just the basics.

Here are some of the basics:

- **Money Market Funds** are considered low-risk, low-return funds. That means they're very safe funds to protect your investment but your investment doesn't grow as quickly in a money market as it might in a different type of fund that has a higher potential for return. Money markets are a great place to put your money if you think you'll need it fairly soon—for a vacation, for example.
- **Income Funds** are just that—funds that provide an income. Income funds invest in what are called fixed-income securities, such as government and corporate bonds and mortgages. These are good funds for people who are seeking a regular income from their investments and generally are a key element of almost any well-balanced investment program.
- **Growth or Equity Funds** invest in stocks (companies) and have a greater potential to grow, over time. These are good funds to invest in if you intend to leave your money in a fund for a long period.
- **Balanced Funds** are a combination of money market, income, and growth funds. These are worthwhile funds to invest in if you're starting out and want some stability mixed with some growth. Fund managers are responsible for the asset-allocation mix in the fund. It's up to them to monitor world money markets and prudently move around or "manage" the asset mix in the fund according to the current market and economic changes.
- **Global Funds** invest in countries around the world. They generally offer higher growth and risk potential than funds invested just in Canada, and can usually tend to offset declines in the Canadian dollar. Conversely, when the Canadian dollar is rising against a foreign currency, the value of the investment will fall. They may invest in money markets, bonds, stocks, or all three. A globally diversified portfolio is usually less volatile than those held in a single country.
- **Index Funds** invest to emulate or track the performance of a particular market index. For example, a number of index funds currently available are invested to track the performance of the TSE 300. They achieve this by investing in the same investments as the index or a representative sample of those investments. They tend to move up or down with Canada's largest stock market.

How are your mutual funds performing?

If you don't want to reply, "Fine thank you, how are yours?" read on. People really do discuss their funds and it's really not all that complicated.

"Performance" just means growth

Sometimes it's steady, slow growth, as in money market funds and income funds. Sometimes your fund takes a big jump up, then a big dip, then a big jump again. Equity funds can sometimes act that way. A fund like that can be described as volatile. Volatility sounds scary but it doesn't have to be.

If you plan to leave your investment where it is for a long time, you shouldn't worry too much about ups and downs. A long-term investment strategy is generally viewed as the best approach. You'll survive the bumps while avoiding the biggest pitfall of "buying high and selling low."

Performance depends on many different factors, including the kind of fund you own and where we are in the economic cycle. All economies move in cycles of expansion and contraction. In each stage of any given cycle, some investments will tend to perform better than others. For instance, in a "recovering economy," companies tend to make larger profits so their stock goes up. So too can interest rates when economic times improve. When that happens, bond prices tend to go down so bond funds generally don't perform as well. In a "high-interest-rate economy," Treasury-Bill investors do well. But, with high interest rates, there's often inflation so T-Bill investors may have less purchasing power with their gain.

Are you dizzy yet? Diversification and risk

One thing is certain: no matter where we are in the economic cycle, at least one asset class will perform better than the others. Since no one can time the cycle accurately enough to be safe all the time, it's best to invest a little in each asset class.

When you spread your investments around in different asset classes, you reduce your risk and increase your long-term growth potential. That's called "diversification" (another key word you can bandy about with your learned friends).

Remember, money market funds are really dependable but are not big growth products. Bonds and mortgage funds can provide income and potential for capital gains. Equity funds that reflect the ups and downs of the stock market represent the potential for higher growth but are also riskier. What's most important is finding the right asset mix for you and your financial future.

Risk and rate of return are big factors in all investment decisions. In most cases, your overall goals, tolerance for risk, and time horizon are considerations that guide you in the right direction. And remember, high growth generally brings high risk.

How to pick 'em

So now you know about funds and what's in them. You know which types of funds are the least risky and which types have the highest potential for growth.

The next step is to match your expectations with your fund choices. That means it's time to determine your "financial profile," which is made up of these factors:

- how much growth you need
- when you need the money
- your tolerance for risk

Some of this may involve some guesswork, but most of us know what kind of lifestyle we have now and have a good idea of what we'd like to have in the future. At the same time, keep in mind that you don't have to peer into a crystal ball all by yourself. Bankers and financial planners who have the training (or know plenty of people who have) can assist you in determining the investments that will most likely help to satisfy your needs, both now and in the future.

Fund managers have style

As you discovered previously here, a fund manager is responsible for "managing" mutual funds. Each manager is in charge of the money that various individuals like you invested in the fund. Except for money market funds, which have a fixed unit price, the "net asset value" (that is, the price of each unit of the mutual fund) fluctuates according to market conditions. Different managers approach such fluctuations in different ways.

The passive manager

Being a passive manager doesn't mean sitting around all day doing nothing. It means that the manager's style of investing is comparatively more conservative. A passive manager manages index funds. She aims to match the returns of a major benchmark index. Believing the theory that it's hard to outguess the markets over the long term, passive managers work with sophisticated computer technology to prove that market prices reflect the knowledge and expectations of all investors. They work to prove that given that pool of knowledge, it's almost impossible to outperform the market averages.

The active manager

Give her a voice and it would probably say, "Yahoo." That's the active fund manager. She likes the challenge of investing and wants to win. That means she wants and believes her funds will outperform the stock markets and other market measurements.

The active manager analyzes companies, financial markets, and economic trends. She examines the potential for big gains and believes her choices will provide better-than-average returns. She bases her investment decisions on careful research and experience.

Investment fees

Mutual funds typically have what is called a management fee. It's usually one of the ways fund managers make their money. Generally speaking, the more complex the fund, the higher the fee. An index fund usually charges the lowest fee. Other operating costs include legal, auditing, and administration fees. Management fees and operating expenses are added together to arrive at what is called the management expense ratio (MER). When you're choosing a fund, you'll want to compare MERs as one criterion. A fund MER is disclosed in the simplified prospectus.

Front, back, and no-loads

Sales charges are commissions called "loads" that we pay to the person or mutual fund company when we buy specific mutual funds. The commission or load is used to pay the person who assisted you in your investment decisions. Since there are several variations, ask the mutual fund company or sales representative to explain how it works.

A "front-end load" is paid at the time of purchase. A "back-end load" may be paid when you sell or cash in your fund. Fees vary widely, but 3 or 4 per cent is fairly common. Funds that are sold directly to the buyer from the fund company have no commissions and are called "no-load funds." These funds are available through banks, insurance companies, and some independent firms. Look for ways to reduce the commissions you pay. The less you pay in fees, the greater your return because you have more to invest.

Track record

Your fund manager has a track record based on her experience in managing her particular fund or group of funds. You can check her record of investments, for the past three to five years—possibly even 10 or more if the fund has been around that long and she's been managing it all that time. If she hasn't been in charge the whole time, overall performance may vary, depending on who was managing the fund. Regardless, you must check over a fairly long period because, in the short term, markets can change dramatically. A good performance picture is likely to include a few years of ups and downs.

What are you looking for? Comparisons. Apples to apples. Compare the fund you're interested in with others like it. For example, you may want to invest in the health care industry. Look for the performance records for mutual funds specializing in that industry to determine who's doing what and how they're doing. The best indication of good performance is the fund's ability to outperform other similar funds.

And don't forget: the past is a good indicator but nobody can predict the future. No fund or fund manager carries any guarantee of how it or she will perform in the future.

And finally, if all this seems like too much information, you can always contact your financial planner to discuss your options.

Will somebody please manage my investments?

So many options. So little time. There must be an easier way to invest.

There is. Some financial institutions now offer asset management programs. They'll help you build your portfolio, monitor your investments, and report back to you on a regular basis.

Managing assets means managing them according to your needs, your goals, and your risk tolerance. A fund manager looks out for you when the market fluctuates so you don't have to worry. Your fund manager will rebalance your portfolio when required and, after notifying you, will make any necessary changes.

In a managed asset program, you won't be left in the dark. You'll usually receive a personalized report of your investments' progress with a clear indication of what has influenced that performance over the relevant period.

Nothing stays the same

Your funds' performance will vary. But you can try to minimize volatility, and take full advantage of diversification and global investments through a managed asset program. These programs can give you greater peace of mind because your fund manager will continually rebalance your portfolio based on stated objectives to continue to meet your goals and needs.

Rebalancing is a reallocation of your money from the most recent better performing investments to the relative underperformers. We've all heard of "buy low, sell high." In a changing market, that's just what a managed-asset program will attempt to achieve for you. During a bull or good market, the equity fund portion of your portfolio may grow and represent a larger portion of your portfolio than planned. To get back to your original asset mix, some of your equity investments will be sold. And when the market is a bear (that's bad), it's often a good time to buy the equity portion of your portfolio.

Aren't you glad there's someone else to do all that juggling?

Saving Strategies

Many people spend a lot of time figuring out how to get the most out of savings. And they've figured out some fairly effective ways to max out your hard-earned income.

Diversification

Spread it around—the risk, that is. As discussed earlier, diversification works on the principle that no single investment works well under all economic conditions. When you spread your investments around, you reduce the impact of one poor performer on your portfolio. In doing that, you also tend to achieve a greater rate of return, in the long term, on your investment than if you had invested only in the safest assets.

Remember the term "risk/return trade off"—that is, the higher the risk, the higher the potential return? The same applies to the lower the risk, the lower the potential return? A portfolio that combines all three asset classes—safety, income, and growth—is considered a diversified portfolio.

You can diversify among asset classes to hedge against changes in the economic cycles. You can diversify within asset classes to compensate for other risks that may vary within that class, such as a company's performance. And you can diversify globally to protect yourself against any downside economic changes in any one country.

Time is money

Long-term investing allows you the advantages of compounding—that is, with a fixed-income investment, interest is paid on your interest. For stocks, it means reinvesting dividends to buy more stocks. When saving for the long term, remember:

- Don't ignore risk; look for investments with long-term growth potential.
- Stay with your investment unless there is a significant change to the investment or to your personal situation—after all, if you cash out sooner than you planned, compounding advantages are lost.
- Start early and invest often; time is the key to long-term growth.

Dollar cost averaging

A little bit goes a long way—if it's done all the time. The key to this strategy is to make a habit of investing even small amounts of money frequently.

If, when you start budgeting, you pay yourself first and get into the habit of doing that consistently over time, you may be amazed at the results.

Quite simply, by investing the same amount in the same investment at regular intervals, you automatically buy more of the investment when prices are low and less when prices are high. That's dollar cost-averaging.

Foreign investing

We're allowed to invest up to 20 per cent of the total cost amount of all investments held in our RRSP accounts in eligible foreign investments. One way to get more exposure to foreign markets is to invest through mutual funds. Not only do global mutual funds qualify as foreign content in your RRSP, but domestic mutual funds that are 100 per cent RRSP-eligible may also invest up to 20 per cent of their assets in foreign investments. Through careful selection, you can increase your global investment without exceeding the RRSP foreign-content limit.

Global investing allows you to diversify among economies and markets that, over time, behave differently from ours. Global markets can also provide greater access to high-growth areas such as technology, entertainment, and telecommunications.

Canada's stock markets represent less than 2 per cent of the world's total market capitalization! This means that 98 per cent of investment opportunities lie outside our domestic borders. But less than half of Canadians take advantage of foreign market investments. Now you know. So look into it. You'll get the most out of your savings when you think and invest strategically.

Maximizing your RRSP

It's great to have a budget and a savings plan but it's important to take a fresh look at it periodically. Even if your retirement seems a lifetime away, the earlier you sock away as much as you can in savings, the better off you'll be.

Remember to take advantage of your high-income years. That means a couple of things. It's the time when you're subject to the highest rate of income tax and the time you should be saving the most. That's why it makes sense to contribute as much as you can into your RRSP. You'll increase your savings and decrease your income tax burden.

How much can I invest?

We all have annual RRSP contribution limits. Basically, you're allowed to contribute up to 18 per cent of your previous year's earned income, to a maximum of $13,500. But, if you have a company pension plan, which means that your company is helping you save for retirement, then your RRSP contribution will be lower. Contribution limits are set by the federal government and won't change until 2004.

Here's the easiest way to determine your contribution limit. Every year, after you've filed your income tax, Revenue Canada will send you a "Notice of Assessment." Your RRSP contribution limit will appear on that notice.

Let's say your last Notice of Assessment indicated that you could contribute $12,000 to your RRSP, but you managed to contribute only $10,000. That means that next year, your contribution limit will increase by the $2,000 you didn't contribute this year. In other words, you can carry forward your allowable contribution limit so that next year, assuming your income is the same, you can contribute $14,000. And, you don't have to use all of your RRSP contributions as deduction in the current year. They can be carried forward indefinitely.

Should I borrow to buy an RRSP?
If you feel you just can't afford to contribute to your RRSP before the annual deadline rolls around, you might want to consider doing what many Canadians do: borrow to contribute to an RRSP.

When you do that, you can take advantage of the tax benefits that come with contributing to RRSPs, you'll get your money working for you, and in the long run, after you've paid the loan, you'll benefit from the savings.

Issues to consider when you borrow to contribute to your RRSP
• Are you comfortable with having a loan that can take years to pay off?
• If making loan repayments prevents you from contributing next year, it may not be a good decision for you.
• It's a *loan*—which means that it's part of your debt/service ratio. In other words, it's money you will continue to pay out monthly. What happens if you need to borrow for another reason? You may be able to get a "consolidation loan" as discussed earlier, but it will mean even higher monthly payments. Keep that in mind.

Saving for two
Spousal RRSPs provide a way for spouses to save for retirement and also save on income tax in retirement. The owner of an RRSP is called the planholder or annuitant. That's you. You pay into it, you own it. On the other hand, a spousal RRSP is an arrangement where one spouse contributes to the RRSP and the other spouse is the planholder.

Apart from being a really generous gal, why would I do that? Good question.

The contributions we make are based on our contribution limit which, as we've seen previously, is related to our annual income. The person who contributes the money (that would be you) receives the tax deduction. Most often, the spouse in the higher tax bracket contributes to a spousal RRSP to benefit from the tax deduction. It's important, however, also to consider what both you and your spouse can anticipate in terms of income at the time of retirement.

A spousal RRSP enables you to "split income" at retirement, meaning that each of you can earn similar amounts. The result is usually lower income taxes in total for the two of you as money is withdrawn (also known as your retirement income). Any funds contributed to a spousal RRSP are considered the property of the spouse in whose name the RRSP is registered—the planholder. He or she must also pay income tax on those funds as they're withdrawn.

There's also this consideration: if funds are withdrawn, the spouse who made the contribution must include in his or her income the amount received by the planholder from the RRSP up to the spouse's contribution for that year and the two previous calendar years. This is called the three-year attribution rule.

When retirement time finally arrives and you need the money you've accumulated in an RRSP, you'll be in a better tax position if each of you has an RRSP of similar amounts. Referred to as "income splitting," it simply means that two people will pay less tax on two smaller RRSPs than one person would pay on a combined amount. Ain't marriage grand?

Group RRSPs
Many companies and associations offer plans for employees or members to contribute as part of a group to an RRSP. If you have a Group RRSP plan in your company, you can decide (just as with automatic withdrawal from your account into your savings) how much you want to invest and how often. Your employer will deduct the amount and you

can decide where to invest it. At the same time, your pay slip will show that your income tax deduction is lower because, with a Group RRSP, your income tax savings are immediate. You don't have to wait until tax time next spring to see your tax savings.

Some generous employers offer plans that help you save. You agree to save a certain amount in an RRSP every month and your generous employer matches that amount. There is a taxable benefit equal to the amount of your employer's contribution. However, you will receive an income tax deduction within your RRSP limit for the same amount. So check out these programs. If your company offers you a plan, find out about it and sign up right away. If your employer doesn't offer a plan, find out if one can be implemented.

RRSPs and taxes

Contributions to an RRSP are deductible for any given year if they are contributed in the year or within 60 days after the end of the year.

- Make contributions early in your working life, and contribute as much as you can.
- Don't wait for the deadline; the earlier in the year you contribute, the earlier you can apply for a reduction of the tax withheld at source by your employer (see your human resources advisor for details).
- Ask your employer to withhold a portion from your pay for direct deposit to an RRSP.
- Consider paying administration fees outside the plan to maximize your future growth.
- Keep track of your unused contribution limit and try to catch up.
- If you're paying alimony or maintenance or have rental income losses, check to see how that may affect your contribution limit.

Whom can I trust?

There are many, many financial experts in the marketplace. Many experts work for institutions like banks, insurance companies, accounting firms, and brokerage houses. Others work independently. Some charge a fee for their services, others do not. It's important to know what your needs are since financial planners are experts in various fields.

It's important to shop around for someone you trust. Start by asking family or friends or work colleagues to suggest someone. Or perhaps you'd like to start by talking to someone at your bank. You're not obligated to stay with someone who doesn't meet your needs or doesn't seem helpful.

It's your future and you'll want to feel comfortable with the person who will help you make critical decisions. Why would you put your financial health in the hands of someone you don't feel comfortable with?

How to choose a financial planner

When you buy a car, you kick the tires. When you buy a house, you check the foundation and the plumbing. And when you choose a financial planner, you must be just as cautious.

It's your money and you must be able to trust the person who's helping you make some pretty big decisions about your future. So treat the process as if you're hiring an employee and ask her a few questions:

• WHAT ARE HER QUALIFICATIONS?
Ask about her background and education. Your planner can take specific courses to increase her knowledge. Check out her walls for diplomas that prove she's earned key designations such as Certified Financial Planner (CFP), Personal Financial Planner (PFP), or Chartered Financial Analyst (CFA).

• HOW WILL SHE DEAL WITH YOU IN GOOD TIMES & BAD?
Optimists are great people, but a good planner should have a plan to address both the ups and the downs in the market.

• HOW IS SHE PAID?
Some planners are paid on commission, some on salary, some on a combination of the two. And some charge a fee based on the value of

your assets. If her fee is related in some way to the kind of investments she's recommending to you, find out that information. After all, it's your money.

• WHAT IS SHE ALLOWED TO SELL?
Some planners can sell only mutual funds. Others can sell only products of one company. If you want a diverse investment portfolio, you should choose someone who can sell a wide range of investments and financial products.

• WHO WATCHES OVER HER?
If there's ever a problem, your advisor's boss is the first place to appeal for help. If you want to conduct a background check, the Investment Dealers Association and other provincial securities regulators keep files that show any complaints against stockbrokers. Also check into the company that the advisor works for, if applicable.

• HOW OFTEN WILL I HEAR FROM YOU?
Part of your comfort level with your planner comes from meeting your expectations. So find out how often she'll call. And make sure she calls if something dramatic happens, such as a big shift in the stock market, and that she's available when you try to contact her.

• WHOM CAN I CALL?
Ask your friends for references. Ask friends who have existing relationships to see if they're satisfied with the service they're receiving.

Am I comfortable?
What it finally comes down to is whether you like working with this person. Do you trust her? Do you like her style? Do you feel comfortable that she's working for your best interests? Trust your instincts.

It's about you

You may feel really comfortable with your planner, but remember—stay involved. Continue to learn more about your investments and you'll find that conversations with your planner will become more interesting and productive.

Kiddy Finances

For many of us, financial responsibilities extend far beyond looking after our own retirement. And that's particularly true when you become a parent.

Having children is a huge responsibility. And they grow up so quickly. With children comes a lifelong obligation not only to love them and teach them but also to consider the cost of raising them in the best way you can. And that takes planning. So even if you don't have children now, and don't plan to, you should read this section. You may be an aunt or a godmother and you can always share some good advice with your family and friends.

One of the greatest responsibilities most of us face is ensuring the best possible educational opportunities for our kids. Post-secondary education is a huge investment. According to recent statistics, if your child attends university for four years, she will have paid at least $16,000, or as much as $40,000 if she goes away from home and needs to stay in residence or in an apartment. Like many good things, the costs continue to rise every year.

There are many reasons to start saving early for the good of your children, and almost as many ways to do it. Here are some suggestions on how you can get started, and get them thinking about it too.

Planting the saving seed

It's a simple fact that sooner rather than later, your children should learn how to save their pennies before they start spending them. Whether you provide an allowance for your child, open a savings account for her, or purchase life insurance, you're teaching her about managing her money. And the earlier the better. You may be surprised to discover that many children take this responsibility very seriously.

Registered Education Savings Plans

Registered Education Savings Plans (RESPs) are one of the most popular ways to save for kids' higher education. These plans are available at most financial institutions, mutual fund companies, and life insurance companies. You can contribute up to $4,000 per year to a maximum of $42,000 per beneficiary.

In the 1998 federal budget, the federal government introduced the Canada Education Savings Grant (CESG) for people saving in an RESP. The program pays a grant into an RESP of 20 per cent of the first $2,000 in annual RESP contributions for each beneficiary under the age of 18 (certain restrictions apply to children age 16 or 17) to a maximum of $400 and a lifetime maximum of $7,200. Unused RESP contribution room can be carried forward, but annual contributions in excess of $2,000 will not attract an additional CESG in any year.

Income on the RESP investments accumulates tax free until it is withdrawn. Unlike with RRSPs, contributions are not tax deductible. When the student receives the income that accumulated on the CESG and contributions, he or she will be taxed on both amounts. The good news is that most students don't have a big income so the tax rate will be relatively low.

If your child decides not to attend a qualifying post-secondary institution, certain conditions currently apply that enable you to transfer the accumulated income in the RESP funds into an RRSP to a lifetime maximum of $50,000. If you don't have enough RRSP contribution room, the income you withdraw will be taxed at 20 per cent, in addition to your regular taxes. Quebec residents will pay an additional 10 per cent tax in this situation. Your original contributions to the RESP are returned tax free and the CESG must be repaid to the government. You may also want to look into the option of designating a different beneficiary, if the plan allows.

Informal trusts

Another simple way to save for children's education is to open a regular (non-registered) investment account, known as an informal trust. The account is in your name "in trust."

- There are no restrictions on the amount you invest or the investments you make.
- You aren't penalized if your child does not attend a post-secondary institution.
- You can take advantage of income splitting. Until your child reaches the age of majority, you must pay tax on any interest or dividend income, while the child pays tax on any capital gains and any income earned on reinvested interest or dividend income.

Once your child reaches the legal age of majority, you can re-register the account in your child's name. From then on, all income is taxable in the child's hands. When she needs the money, a convenient monthly withdrawal plan can be set up to cover regular expenses.

Life insurance for children

Most people who don't know why we should buy life insurance for children think it's an absolutely gruesome idea. That's because nobody wants to consider the possibility of losing a child. Unfortunately, however, it does occasionally happen and when it does, life insurance can help cover unexpected expenses. There are several other important and very good reasons to buy life insurance for children.

Guaranteed insurability

When you purchase life insurance for your child, you're helping her on the road to financial security. Your child becomes the insured on her policy and may, at predetermined intervals, purchase more insurance without having to submit to any medical exams.

Life insurance for higher learning

Life insurance can be a great way to pay for college or university. When you buy a permanent policy for your child, the savings build over time, while the monthly premium remains the same. If you start early, for as little as $25 a week, a fund could be ready for your child when she's ready to take the big step. By the time your child is ready to attend university, that little investment will be there to help provide the cost of her education. If she decides not to pursue higher learning, the funds, unlike some other plans, are still there to use in other ways. Be sure to check out the tax implications.

Just invest it

Yet another way to save for university is to set up a pre-authorized purchase plan. If your child will be attending university in 10 years and you estimate that she'll need a total of $25,000 over four years, you'll need to start saving $140 a month. If you have a new baby and you start right now, you'll only have to save $80 a month to have enough when your baby is a young adult, ready for university.

An investment of $100 a month, earning 8 per cent annual effective rate of return, will grow to $33,978 over 15 years. Of course, the higher the return, the less time it will take to save. You don't want to put these important funds at too much risk, but a long-term growth fund is a good idea for maximum growth potential.

On-line Decisions

It's amazing. The World Wide Web was born in 1991. In 1993 there were 130 web sites. By 1999, that number had grown to over two million.

You can shop and buy almost anything on the Net from books to music, from clothes to antiques. And you can buy financial services. Most banks and financial institutions now have web sites. And a full range of financial services are available at the touch of the mouse.

When it comes to mutual funds, you can watch the growth of your fund, research new ones, have a look at historical performance. You'll find out about asset mix, fund performance, fund track records. You can review your investment options, download applications, and apply for products and services on-line.

But, as with everything concerned with your future, be cautious and do your research. Make sure the web site you visit is owned by a reputable, legitimate group. And be careful about the promises made for huge gains. You might be disappointed.

There's so much to think about when you're dealing with your future. And the more you know, the better off you'll be. Each bit of knowledge you acquire can bring you closer to your financial goals and closer to a peaceful, more balanced life.

Take the time to continue to learn more.

Financial Health Check-up

To summarize how you're doing so far, keep the following checklist in mind as you measure your progress in getting closer to more balanced financial health.

THE "LEARN MORE, EARN MORE" CHECKLIST

Completion date

- I know about debt and equity securities. _____
- I understand what asset classes are. _____
- I know about mutual funds and how they perform. _____
- I understand how the economy affects the
  performance of my funds. _____
- I understand the principle of risk and return. _____
- I know what index funds are. _____
- I know what fund managers do and how they do it. _____
- I'm aware of the investment fees I have to pay. _____
- I know how my investment fee is calculated. _____
- I understand managed asset programs. _____
- I'm aware of important savings strategies. _____
- I know how a spousal RRSP works. _____
- I've checked to see if my employer offers
  a group RRSP plan. _____
- I know how to find a financial planner I can trust. _____
- I know why it's important for children to
  have life insurance. _____
- I know the best ways to save for my child's
  education and I am saving. _____
- I'm aware there are lots of financial tips on the
  Internet and I use it to increase my knowledge. _____

Personal Perspectives on the Challenges of Achieving a Richer, More Fulfilling Lifestyle

As you meet the following individuals and understand their personal situations, you may see elements of yourself at a certain age or stage of your life.

Following each woman's story are constructive suggestions on how she might deal with the challenges she's facing today. Some of these pointers might also relate to you and your ability to enhance your chance to achieve greater balance and personal fulfillment.

Karen

Age:	37 (partner, no children)
Occupation:	Teacher

FINANCIAL SNAPSHOT

Karen's Assets		*Liabilities*	
Condo	$210,000	nil	
Car	$6,000		
Savings	$3,000		
RRSPs	$3,000		
Sailboat	$1,750		
Total Assets:	$223,750	Total Liabilities:	nil
Estimated Net Worth:	$223,750		

Estimated Cash Flow

Net Monthly Income $2,000

Karen's Key Monthly Expenses

Investment Programs	$45
Household Expenses	$800
Mortgage/Rent	$nil
Insurance Plans	$85
Debt Payments	$nil

Monthly Expenses (cont'd)
Discretionary Expenses $200
Travel $800

Total Income $2,000

Total Expenses $1,930

Personal snapshot

"My partner and I live well and we want to continue to live well. I teach high school French and Colin teaches social work at the local community college. We both have pensions, savings, and RRSPs. I'm also able to get freelance work as a coach in French.

"We're also into real estate. We live in a condo I bought with the money I made from my first condo and that was bought with a legacy from my father. Colin and I share the income from his house, which is rented out. We've discussed selling his house and this condo, and then buying a "fixer-upper" in a better neighbourhood that we'd renovate. I would like to buy a cottage because I've learned that northern vacation properties are growing in value as baby boomers age.

"We share all expenses, and when summer comes, we take off. We've gone to Europe, Asia, Africa, and Australia over the past seven years during our summer vacations. Mostly, we backpack. It's cheaper and more fun. One year, we climbed Mount Rainier. We've met the greatest people this way. I try to run at the fitness centre at least three times a week. And I have a small sailboat that we trail out to the nearby lakes.

"Yes, it's a great life. But then my bank gave me a computer program to run on our PC. We fed in our financial details and the program told us that we weren't saving nearly enough for retirement. We were both shocked. Of course, our real estate didn't count for much because who knows what it will be worth when we come to sell. I can tell you, it was a real wake-up call.

"We'd been coasting along thinking we were in secure, union-protected jobs and that we both had good pensions. Then we realized that this was no longer as true as it once was. Friends have left the profession, older teachers are accepting buy-out packages. There's change in the air. I went into teaching because it offered long-term security as well as a rewarding job. Now it may not be there for me in a few years. I'm not too old to change professions, but the idea of change will take some getting used to."

FQ rating: B

Considerations: It's easy to forget that approximately a quarter of the working population is paid by the government. Now all governments are changing their priorities, and jobs that were once secure no longer look that way. Like many in the private sector, public servants are feeling nervous and expressing more concern about their future.

What's happening to your RRSPs? Are you not maximizing your contributions? I assume you have some life insurance through group plans. Risk management is a key component of a comprehensive financial plan, and this is just what I think you'd better work on. You don't have to do it alone. I would suggest that you and Colin discuss your joint goals with a financial advisor.

The computer program provided by the bank was obviously an overdue wake-up call, but there's nothing like talking to a person. Your bank can recommend someone who will know what options are available to you—particularly the best way to save while minimizing your tax situation. Saving sounds so simple, but today there are several different ways to do it and an expert can help guide you through this maze. Suggestion: for just one month, keep track of every expense you incur— every one. I have a feeling you'll find that your expenses are considerably higher than you think.

Pearl

Age: 51 (Married/five children)
Occupation: Housemaid

FINANCIAL SNAPSHOT

Pearl's Assets		*Liabilities*
Savings	$15,200	Total Liabilities nil

Total Assets $15,200

Estimated Net Worth: $15,200

Pearl's Estimated Cash Flow
Net Monthly Income $1,100

Key Monthly Expenses
Investment Programs $50
Household Expenses $600
Mortgage/Rent $nil
Insurance Plans $nil
Debt Payments $nil
Discretionary Expenses $200

Total Income $1,100
Total Expenses $850

Personal snapshot

"Jerry and I emigrated to Canada 20 years ago, and we've never regretted it. Sure, it's been hard raising five kids in the city, but they're going to make it. Jerry's a clerk with the city, and he's got a pension coming. I'd like to stay home with the kids. The eldest is 16, the youngest is 6, but we don't have the cash. I work as a maid for a big maid service.

"Sometimes I pick up extra work from this woman, Mrs. Lindhurst, and she gives me clothes for the kids. And Mr. Lindhurst, he sold Jerry the family's old station wagon. Jerry pays him when he can. When Mrs. Lindhurst has a party, she calls me: 'Pearl, only you can help me get the house in order.' That's a whole day's work and I get extra. I'd like to do this more. I have a friend who thinks we should set up a maid service together. Maybe.

"I get $9 an hour from the maid service plus anything I get from freelancing, I save. Always done it. Jerry has some kind of education plan for the kids. It's Jerry who thinks we spend $1,000 a month on food and things for the house and kids, but I really think it's more. There always seems to be something extra. Jerry hates me doing it, but there are times when, okay sure, I've gone to the food bank. You try to keep teenaged boys fed. Just the other day, the head of the school asked me to come in and see her. Was I scared. I thought one of the kids was in trouble. But all she wanted to say was that our 10-year-old Henry needed help with reading. She suggested one of those learning centres. I worked double for a month to get the money together.

"Jerry pays the rent and he has an old car. I don't drive. Michelle, our eldest, helps out in a beauty shop nearby, and she gives me some money when she can. Jerry's been after me to put my savings into RRSPs—that's what he does—but I don't like the idea that I won't be able to get at the money when I want it. Well yes, I play the lottery, five, six bucks a week, and I've won $10 I don't know how many times. If I won big, what wouldn't I do! I dream about a house, clothes for the kids, a trip back home...and not worrying about the rent.

"Retirement? Jerry can retire, but I guess I'll keep working 'til I drop. Exercise? Diet? Michelle does all that. And she's after me to go the community centre for some classes. If I have time, I say."

FQ rating: B

Considerations: Pearl, you've got a little gold mine in your savings account. Congratulations. You are a real Canadian. We used to be the biggest savers in the world. I'm glad to say that I know there are others like you—women who are working for relatively low pay but who still manage to put something away each month.

I think you really might consider putting some of your savings in RRSPs. Would you like to talk to a financial advisor? Your bank can give you a great deal of information about RRSPs and how they help you when you do retire. Maybe you should also ask about a spousal RRSP to consider the benefits of income splitting at retirement. I agree that it's very important to consider an investment mix that will still keep some money in your savings account as a safety cushion for emergencies.

I think you would be very wise to start exercise classes. You've got an active job and it's important for you to stay fit. Exercise not only keeps you flexible but it can lead to greater relaxation—a concept that (it sounds to me) you might think about in terms of your overall approach to a balanced life. Remember that old saying: "all work and no play…"

Mia

Age:	22 (single)
Occupation:	Waitress

FINANCIAL SNAPSHOT

Assets		*Liabilities*	
nil		Student Loan	$12,000
Total Asset:	nil	Total Liabilities:	$12,000

Estimated	
Net Worth:	-$12,000

Estimated Cash Flow

Net Monthly Income	$1,300

Key Monthly Expenses

Investment Programs	$nil
Household Expenses	$520
Mortgage/Rent	$650
Insurance Plans	$nil
Debt Payments	$nil
Discretionary expenses	$130
Total Income	$1,300
Total Expenses	$1,300

Personal snapshot

"I'm going to have a wonderful life. And to make sure of that, I have committed myself to a rigorous five-year schedule. I'm working toward a diploma in medical radiation therapy. My day starts at 7 a.m. and after class, I just have time to get to Vaucluse, an expensive downtown French restaurant by 3.30 p.m. I've been a waitress there for the past year.

"It's hard physical work. I clean the restaurant and help set the tables before the customers start arriving at 5.30 p.m. After the last customer is gone, I have to help clean up. I don't usually get home until midnight. I work six days a week and get paid just over $6 an hour. On good days I work eight hours, on days when the restaurant is doing little business, I may get sent home after two hours. Luckily, the customers are high-end, so I do get good tips on weekends, and that's what I live on.

"A waiter's job is full of pressure—from the kitchen and from customers. That's why I go to yoga once a week. Most days I try to grab an hour to swim at the health club, sometimes as early as 6 a.m.

"Schoolwork is also demanding. I'm going to have been in school for an awful long time before I get my diploma. The total cost will be more than $20,000, but I received a bursary from the college, and I've been able to get a loan too. I'm guessing that I will owe about $12,000, but I'm not worried. The entry pay for a technician is around $39,000, and Canadian-trained technicians have a good reputation, so I'll be able to travel if I want. I'm thinking of going to Australia or the Persian Gulf.

"I don't have enough time for a relationship, even for friends. On Monday, my day off, I do the laundry, shop, and go to yoga. I have to pay for my own uniform, black trousers, black vest, and white cotton shirt. I have my hair done every week, and I have a monthly appointment with an aesthetician. Well, I've got to look good for my job."

FQ rating: B

Considerations: I'm impressed by your motivation and I'm even more impressed by your ability to stay focused on your long-term goal. Yoga is a great idea. Swimming too. I guess you just don't have time for any social life at school or for dating and friends. But you only go around once in this life, Mia, so you might want to give a little bit of thought to your social calendar. Again, I admire your ability to delay gratification, but I have to say that to keep a better balance, I'd like to see you fitting a little more fun into your life—somehow!

To get a good job today, young people are having to stay in school longer and run up bigger debts. The training for a medical radiation technician used to be 28 months. Now you tell me it's much longer. This is a big commitment. To be trained and then pay off the cost of that training could take up to 10 years of your life. Paying off that debt will be a chore, but repayment plans can be structured many different ways and still may enable you to get started on your own personal investment plan. Even if it's just putting aside the tips from a weekend night into an RRSP. Starting now—even small—will pay off big-time years down the road.

You should be aware that Revenue Canada recently introduced a new tax credit for interest on student loans. Check it out and you'll find it will definitely save you some money when you do your tax return. Finally, you must be dealing with a financial institution of some kind. Wherever you have your bank account, go there and see what they have to offer in terms of special student products and services.

Portia

Age:	42 (married with three children)
Occupation:	Internet provider service technician

FINANCIAL SNAPSHOT

Family Assets		Liabilities	
House	$235,000	Credit Card Debt	$4,000
Car	$10,000	Mortgage	$150,000
Savings	$7,000	Home Improvement	
		Loan	$5,000
RRSPs	$5,000		
Total Assets:	$257,000	Total Liabilities:	$159,000

Estimated
   Net Worth: $98,000

Portia's Estimated Cash Flow
Net Monthly Income $1,750

Key Monthly Expenses
Investment Programs $45
Household Expenses $600
Mortgage/Rent $600
Insurance Plans $nil
Debt Payments $230
Discretionary Expenses $175

Total Income $1,750
Total Expenses $1,650

Personal snapshot

"I started out at school knowing I was latching on to the future—computers. I was serious, dedicated, came top of my class in exams and spent my spare time fiddling around with what might now be regarded as antique CPUs. I wanted to go into software design, but then I got married and put that goal on hold. Still, I've kept up with IT (information technology). Right now I'm a part-time service technician at an Internet service provider. It takes a lot of patience. I talk to up to 50 people during my six-hour shift. Most common problem? Getting on to the Web.

"The biggest issue in my life is my recent brush with cancer. I wake up at night in terror that I'll be unable to work—and then what will we all do? One night I got up and rewrote my will. People keep telling me that eventually I'll see it as a wake-up call to really make every minute of my life count. I believe there is time. I'm just not there yet.

"Cancer skews a family, I've read lots about it and I've been in therapy. But the family is still in shock. We were doing okay when it hit.

Emotionally, I mean, not so much financially. I wasn't saving enough and I was relying too much on credit cards to solve my immediate cash needs. But you know how it is with kids, there's always something. We have a great house in the suburbs and a few years ago, we renovated. We're still paying off the loan. But Jim and I agreed it was a good investment.

"The house is in my name, and Jim's got a pension and life insurance, so I felt very secure. Jim earns $15,000 a year more than I do, but we shared expenses equally because he pays for the house and car insurance, and for our holidays. Now he's paying more. We've been discussing whether I should try to get disability insurance. I'll bet it'll be so very expensive, if it's possible.

"I'm worried about getting the kids through university. We don't have an education fund. Jim's always said that he didn't think they should go to university unless they know what they want a degree for. I believe university opens up the world—it certainly did for me. I know I'm going to have to fight for that. I just wish I was in a better financial situation to do so.

"I'd like to work more, but Jim doesn't want me too. Actually, at the moment, I feel happiest at work because I know exactly what I have to do."

FQ rating: B

Considerations: You've got lots on your mind right now, Portia. Lots of women change their lifestyle and life decisions after a major illness. I think many women feel just as you do about being able to focus on work—compared to the emotional upheaval at home. It's difficult to get over this kind of shock.

All things considered, I really think you've been doing better than you think—but that's only from what I can see based on what you've told me about the total family picture. Most importantly, any mom can understand what it's like to keep up with the kids. One thing you really have going for you is that you, unlike some women your age, are computer-literate. There are fresh opportunities all the time in this field.

I think that as you feel better, you may want to explore them, particularly applications that you might be able to address at home. That could enable you to have a more flexible work schedule without giving up family time.

You've made a good start with RRSPs and savings, but you need to stay focused if you're going to live comfortably in retirement. Looking toward a secure retirement is something else. Would it be a good idea for you and Jim to talk to someone at your bank about the best way to coordinate your savings and investments into a long-term retirement plan? Having this goal might make you feel better all around.

Would it be worth exploring whether your children might be eligible for bursaries at university? And remember, there are student loans available.

Because you've been ill, I think you owe it to yourself to set some specific priorities. Have you and Jim talked at all with a financial advisor or someone at the bank about estate planning? Should the house be in your name? If something did happen to you, it would cause additional cost if the house wasn't in both your names. I also think you might talk to an insurance specialist about whether there is some form of insurance available to you.

5 Maxing Out
Your Investments

Financial Tips for Women Who've Come a Long Way

What a score: between 40 and 56! You've been doing your financial homework. Now let's see where we can make some improvements, fill some holes, and solidify your investment in you.

Think about your house or your apartment. You move in, you set up, you decorate. Everything's to your taste. Your living space is comfortable and attractive. But that doesn't mean you can't make some changes along the way. Minor adjustments could improve the investment in your home and make you feel even more comfortable. Your financial health works that way too.

You've done well so far and you've made a point of learning how to get the most out of your investments. Is there something you've forgotten? Have you prepared for life surprises? Have you named a beneficiary for your estate?

Perhaps you've left a number of your financial decisions to someone else and now you'd like to take a more active role in your savings and investment plans. You're the kind of woman who wants to get the most out of life. Why not make sure you're getting the most from your financial plan?

After you've gone through the tips for savvy women like you, have a look at the stories of other women with similar quiz scores. Their situations and the advice they're given may ring a bell or two.

Ready to retire?

Although you may not be ready to retire right now, you should be planning for it. It's never too early or too late to think about your retirement. If you are convinced that you've delayed your financial planning for too long and are now overwhelmed at the thought of retirement, you must take a hard look at where you are and begin today to take action. Great advice, right? But where to start?

It could be that a lot of your anxiety about retirement is that you are in the dark about how to prepare for it. Don't worry. There are professionals who can and will help you to make wise choices.

Once you've found a financial planner you like and trust to help you prepare for retirement, you'll need to get some information to help her do the math. Armed with your financial facts, your planner can show you how to calculate where you are today and help you to plan for where you want to be tomorrow. Here are a few things you'll need to know right now:

Company pension plans

Many companies offer some sort of pension plan. If you're not sure of the details, ask someone in your company, perhaps in your human resources department, to explain what kind of plan your company offers. There will also be records detailing where your plan is today.

If you have worked for more than one company, be sure to have all of the paperwork from all of the companies you worked for. If your company has brochures explaining employee plans, pick those up too. Your financial planner needs to know all of your options.

A "defined benefit plan" is administered by your employer. The retirement benefit you may be entitled to is based on a formula that takes into consideration your income, your job classification and the number of years you've been working for the company. The contribution that you or your employer (or both of you) make is based on a percentage of your salary.

With a "defined contribution plan" or "money purchase plan," your retirement benefit is based on contributions made over the course of your working years and available at your retirement.

Sometimes the employer sets a percentage of your income to be contributed. Sometimes you—the employee—contributes and your employer matches your contribution. Sometimes the employer determines where the funds will be invested and sometimes the employee can make the investment decisions.

With all of those options, it's important to find out exactly how your company's plan works and ask your financial planner to determine the income you could receive at retirement.

And don't forget to check whether your company has a Group RRSP plan. It could represent a significant chunk of your retirement income.

Government pension plans

Your financial planner can help you determine what you are entitled to receive from the government upon retirement. Government plans include the following:

• **Canada Pension Plan or Quebec Pension Plan (CPP/QPP)** These plans provide a monthly retirement income to all retirees who have contributed to the plan for at least one year. You may be eligible to start collecting at age 65 or as early as age 60 provided you can show you "substantially" ceased to be a paid employee and earn less than the maximum annual CPP payable at age 65. You'll receive 0.5% less each month. Or, you can delay receiving payment until age 70 and receive 0.5% more a month. CPP payments are based on a percentage of the income you earned over the years you were contributing to the plan and, of course, the age you decide to collect.

Many people mistakenly believe that benefits from the Canada Pension Plan alone will look after them in retirement. It is important to find out just how much you are entitled to. To some people this information comes as a bit of a shock.

Find out just how much CPP you can expect by contacting Human

Resources Development Canada, which will be listed in the blue pages of the phone book. Once you know that, you can start looking at other sources of income you'll have to add to your CPP benefit.

Periodically, the federal government sends you a statement of your contributions to the CPP and the benefits you can expect to receive at retirement. You may be able to obtain a similar document from the Quebec government QPP benefits.

- **Old Age Security (OAS)** Maximum OAS benefits are paid by the federal government to Canadians over age 65 who have lived in Canada for 40 years after their 18th birthday or who have lived in Canada for 10 consecutive years before applying for the benefit. Supplements are available for low-income Canadians and there are income tax payment requirements for people who have a healthy income from other sources. Based on your income picture, your planner can determine how much OAS benefit you are entitled to receive.

Other savings you can tap into

Once you've given your planner all the facts about your company pension plan and she has filled you in on CPP and OAS, it's time to discuss your other potential income sources. You may be surprised to discover that you're better off than you thought you were.

You've been saving in an RRSP and other savings vehicles for many years. Those savings will play a large part in your retirement income.

If you're a homeowner, you'll need to know how much equity you have in your home. "Equity" essentially means cashable value. Your financial planner, perhaps with the help of a real estate assessor, can determine what your home is worth on the market today.

How do you know how much you'll need?

Retirement planning isn't just about money. It's about what you plan to do when you retire and stop earning a regular income. Retirement planning includes what kind of lifestyle you imagine. Your financial planner will help you determine how much you need to save but first, you must know what lifestyle you want.

Do you want to travel to all the places you've never been? Do you want to spend six months of the year in a warmer climate? Or do you look forward to a quiet life, having your grandchildren over to visit and your friends to play bridge?

Once you've imagined yourself in retirement, your financial planner will help you to figure out what income you'll need. Together you will determine your Canada Pension Plan, Old Age Security, company pension plan(s), assets available for retirement like the equity in your home and any other savings such as savings accounts, mutual funds, Canada Savings Bonds, RRSPs, and insurance policies with a cash value.

Through these calculations, your planner will help you to see how many more years you have to save and how much you will have to save at a given time to get the retirement income you'll need.

The dreaded gap

A gap in your teeth can be charming. A gap in your retirement savings plan can be scary. What's a gap? Quite simply, it's the difference between what you have in accumulated retirement savings, company pension, and government benefits at retirement and what you'll need to support your lifestyle.

Some experts say you'll need 60 to 80 per cent of pre-retirement income to live in retirement with the same lifestyle you enjoyed before you retired. The gap is the difference between that estimate and what you expect you'll have.

Obviously, the earlier you start figuring out your retirement income, the more time you'll have to make up any difference. No matter how much or how little time you have, knowing what you need to fill the gap makes the task much less difficult.

If you have a gap, your planner will offer a number of solutions for you to consider, including some of the following:

- increase your RRSP contributions to increase your savings and defer your income tax
- take advantage of your RRSP contributions but be careful to limit your overcontribution to a maximum of $2000 or you'll pay a 1 per cent penalty per month on the overcontribution above $2000
- when you're about to retire and you have an overcontribution, you'll need to reduce your current contribution to avoid double taxation
- maximize your investment growth by choosing the right mix of investments for you
- change your lifestyle to spend less now and save more for later
- look at ways you could turn a hobby into part-time work
- sell your home at retirement to generate income from investing your equity

Many of us will live a long, healthy life after we stop working. It can be a wonderful time of life if you plan ahead. So don't delay planning for retirement any longer. Certainly don't put it off because you don't know what to do. Remember, there are no stupid questions. Ask someone who knows.

Your saving days are over

It may be a long time before you have to think about spending your retirement income. But it can't hurt to plan ahead with every aspect of your finances.

Your RRSPs won't last forever. The government requires that you "roll them over" by December 31 of the year you turn age 69. These requirements or "transition rules" mean that you'll have to decide what to do with those funds. There are several options:

- you can transfer your RRSP to a RRIF
- you can purchase an annuity
- you can collapse the RRSP, take the cash, and pay the income tax
- you can use a combination of all three options

What's a RRIF?

A Registered Retirement Income Fund (RRIF) has many of the advantages of an RRSP. It's a product that allows you to continue to defer taxes owing on your savings. But, you must withdraw a minimum amount of the money from a RRIF each year, as income. There is no maximum. The amount of money you must withdraw depends on your age. And, of course, you must pay tax on that income.

RRIFs also offer a wide variety of investment opportunities that fall within the three asset classes. You can continue to diversify your portfolio, rebalancing your investments between safety, income, and growth asset classes, as well as taking advantage of the 20 per cent foreign-content rule.

You're allowed, at any time, to move your money around in a RRIF, from one type of investment to another, but you're not allowed to put any more money into it.

What's an annuity?

An annuity provides a regular income of a fixed amount over a specified time period or for the rest of your life, depending on which option you choose, how much income you need, and how much you have invested in your RRSP.

There are a few different kinds of annuities:

- **Term annuities** are set up for a specified period, from 6 to 25 years. The term you choose will depend a lot on how long you expect to need a regular income. Usually that means for the rest of your life. Since we don't know when we're going to die, a little guesswork and calculating will be involved. The risk in determining a term is you could live longer than the term. So if you select a fixed-term annuity, choose wisely. And remember to take inflation into consideration. It could reduce your purchasing power. The lower the inflation rate, the further your money goes.
- **Lifetime annuities** last as long as you do. They cost more, of course, because even the experts don't know how long you'll live. If you live

to be 110, you'll beat the odds. But if you die early, what's left of your money stays with the financial institution.

- **Guaranteed annuities** pay you an income for life. If there's any money left after you die, your beneficiaries receive it.
- **Indexed annuities** pay out at a rate that's adjusted for inflation. If the cost of living goes up, so will your annuity payment.

Annuity payments help you to predict exactly how much retirement income you'll have. But the growth rate of your savings is determined by the financial institution from which you "buy" your annuity. You have no control over where your money is invested. You should discuss the pros and cons of RRIFs and annuities with your financial planner.

Cash 'em out

You can cash in your RRSP and invest the proceeds in something else, but you should figure out if the income tax you'll have to pay makes it worth doing that. You might have to pay more in taxes than you'll earn in interest down the road.

You may want to consider starting your retirement with a RRIF. Then later on, you could move it into an annuity. Or, you could plan, with the help of your financial planner, to exercise a combination of all three options.

To My Loyal Servants, I Leave...

Estate planning

Many people think "estate" means Windsor Castle. What it really means is "your property"—not just your house and property, but all of your earned assets, savings, investments, life insurance, and real estate, as well as all your "stuff" and all your debts. Everybody has some sort of estate and that's why it's really important to plan what you want to do with it.

Rule number one: You can't take it with you. If you accept that, take the next step. Have you planned on what will happen to your estate when you're no longer here? No, it's not a morbid thought. It's reality. Estate planning is the process of getting organized so that you don't leave a mess and a lot of expenses behind for your loved ones to deal with. And it's ultimately to ensure that those whom you intend to receive your assets, actually will.

Probate fees

If you think "pay until you die" is an accurate statement, surprise! You even pay after you die when your will goes through "probate"—a legal process to confirm the validity of your will including who you have appointed executor.

Probate fees are usually based on the size of the estate. They generally apply to the total value of the assets of the estate, without any deductions for outstanding debts on the property, with the exception of outstanding mortgages. Probate fees will vary from province to province. In response to the Supreme Court of Canada's decision in *Re Eurig*, which held that probate fees as previously imposed in Ontario were invalid, the Ontario government introduced the Estate Administration Tax. The new tax mimics the old probate fee rate: 1.5 per cent of the value of probatable assets.

Death and taxes

Your executor is required by Revenue Canada to file your last income tax return within six months of your death or by April 30, whichever comes later.

- Registered Retirement Savings Plans (RRSPs) will generally be treated as though you cashed them in just before your death. They'll be taxed as your income. If you name your spouse or your dependent children as the beneficiary, your RRSPs become the property of that person and avoid probate. This may also result in the deferral of income tax.

- Growth in non-registered assets such as stocks, mutual funds, and vacation homes, other than matrimonial homes, are taxed as capital gains—the difference in fair market value from the time of purchase to the time of death.
- Foreign tax usually applies to real property, investments or businesses outside of Canada. If you have a place in Florida, your estate pays capital gains in both Canada and the United States, as well as American estate tax. However, some of the U.S. taxes may be creditable against the Canadian taxes payable.

There's more. Your estate must also settle and pay for:

- outstanding mortgages
- car loans
- credit card debt
- line of credit
- your funeral
- any other outstanding debts

Really good reasons to have a will

Whose life was it anyway? Yours, of course. That's why it just makes sense to organize your thoughts, and your life, and let the people you love know how you want things to be—and save them money and heartache.

If you die without a will (that is, "intestate"), the court will appoint an administrator who will make decisions about your assets, according to a rigid statutory formula or the needs of your dependants.

What a cruel irony it would be to have this happen, after you spent all that time and energy investing in you and your family. Are you convinced yet? Okay, let's get started.

There are three common types of wills

- A conventional or formal will is valid in all Canadian provinces. It's put together by a lawyer, according to your wishes. You work with the lawyer to determine exactly what you want. Then the will is signed by two witnesses. The witnesses can't be the same people who benefit from the will.

- A notorial will is valid only in Quebec and is read to you by the notary in the presence of two other notaries. The notary keeps the original.

- A holograph will is valid in some provinces, not others. This is a will that is handwritten and dated by you. But it's a bit risky because if there's anything in your will that's not quite clear, the lawyers may have to become involved to figure out what you meant. And that can cause delays.

Put someone in charge

The first thing you must do is choose an executor. Your executor or estate trustee is the person or company who will take care of business after you die. The executor will ensure that things happen the way you wanted them to happen.

The executor you choose can be your partner, your adult child, a friend, or a trust company. Whoever it is, the executor should understand the responsibility. She should know what will be required of her. Executors are entitled to charge a reasonable fee for their service.

What if you change your mind?

People change and so do our decisions. After you've drawn up your will, with limited exceptions you can change anything at any time by adding a "codicil." That means you change a sentence or a paragraph without having to write a whole new will. Just inform your lawyer that you want to make a change and she'll look after it.

Power of attorney

Long before you die, you may be incapacitated by illness or accident and be unable to make important decisions. Although it's grim to think about such things, they do happen and, like so many other unpleasant events, it's best to be prepared for them just in case. When you appoint a person with "power of attorney," you're trusting that person to make decisions for you in case you're unable to. You can appoint your partner, an adult child, a friend, or a trust company.

Here's why it's so important. If you can't sign cheques or go to the bank or pay your bills and you haven't appointed someone to act for you, nothing will get done. Your assets will be locked up, waiting for you to do something. And, if you have people depending on you, there's nothing they can do except apply to the court for the power to act, unless you've given someone legal permission to take care of your financial business. You don't need a lawyer, in most provinces, to appoint someone, but it's a good idea to have a professional review the document to ensure that everything's clear.

Be careful whom you appoint. A power of attorney is a very powerful tool and gives permission to the appointee to do whatever you can do, except make a will.

Living wills

A power of attorney for property takes care of your property. A living will takes care of you. It's a document that outlines what you want regarding your medical care in case you're unable to make decisions about your health care. Some provinces allow you to appoint an attorney to make personal care decisions.

Bury me out on the lone prairee

Don't let the people you love try to guess how you'd like to leave this world. You may not want to think about your funeral but if you do, you'll spare others the pain of making what is really your decision. And be sure to include this information in your will.

Pay now, die later

Remember, it's important to think about these things because whatever you can do to lessen the pain of your death for the people you care about is a loving and generous act. You can plan your funeral in advance so that when you die and your family is in mourning, they'll know exactly what you wanted. You can also arrange everything in advance and pre-pay your funeral. Your will should contain all the details and costs so that no one must guess what's been done and what needs to be done.

Other estate planning techniques

Here are some ways others have dealt with their property. There are advantages and disadvantages to each. Before you proceed, check with a financial planner.

- Choose your beneficiary on RRSPs, RRIFs, and life insurance policies. It's this simple. If you've completed the beneficiary section of these assets, they will go to the person you named. Depending on who the beneficiary of these assets is, they may still be taxable. If no one has been named, your assets will revert to your estate and will be subject to the terms of your will, as well as any applicable taxes and probate fees. The smaller your estate, the less your family will have to pay in probate fees.
- Some people register property jointly with right of survivorship. Both parties are considered owners and both are responsible for the joint property. When one dies, the other becomes the owner of the property. Income tax will still apply on your share of any accrued gain on the property at your death. Contact an advisor to discuss the tax consequences of this strategy.
- Some people give property away to their family or a charity of their choice. If you don't require property, don't wait to pass it on. If you know you'll be leaving your adult children a significant amount of money, consider giving it to them now. Even though tax attribution rules state that you must report any income (except capital gains) earned on money you give to your spouse or children under the age of 18, adult children who receive a cash gift are responsible for paying tax on any income earned on the gift. And remember, if you gift property to your children, you will pay income tax as if you sold the property to them. A gift to charity will give you a nice tax break while you're around to enjoy it, as well as lower estate costs for your

family. A deemed disposition of property may also result in more income, in addition to the donation tax credit. Further details can be obtained from the planned giving office of your favourite charity.

Life insurance has numerous benefits

We all know life insurance pays an amount of money to a beneficiary or the estate at the time of death of the insured. Life insurance is most important when your family needs money to replace your income, pay debts, or fund an education. But, buying life insurance to protect your estate is a great idea for many reasons:

- Life insurance death benefits are generally not taxable. Your estate will receive a lump sum of money that they may use to help them pay debts and other costs of administering your estate. If you buy enough life insurance to cover your funeral costs, debts, estate taxes, and probate fees, your family will be able to receive all of the inheritance you intended them to have.
- Life insurance proceeds can provide your estate with funds for a final gift to charity. If you buy a life insurance policy that names your favourite registered charity as a beneficiary, you can receive a tax credit for the premiums you pay while you're alive.
- You can protect your business and your business partners by purchasing life insurance to fund the purchase of your ownership interest from your estate. When you do, your business can continue to operate and remain profitable, without burdening your family or your business partner. Make sure your partners also buy some.

Discuss life insurance with your children or your heirs. If you can't afford the premiums, maybe it's in your children's best interests to pay them for you.

Naturally, it's not a simple task to think about or act on all these things. And we'd really prefer not to. Yet when we face life's realities and prepare for what eventually will happen, the result is a little bit of that peace of mind we're all trying to achieve.

Boost Your Entrepreneurial Spirit

So you're on your own now! You've flown the corporate coop and decided to do what you've always wanted to do—run your own show. Although it can be scary, when it all comes together self-employment can be a truly satisfying working experience.

Apart from the obvious advantages you appreciate about being self-employed, such as answering the phone in your PJs and doing your work without wearing any make-up, other benefits are to be derived from being self-employed.

When you're self-employed, you can name your own hours. You can work days or nights or both. You can spend your lunch hour planting flowers. And you'll just love your boss (that would be you). But there's more.

It's not for the timid

When considering the benefits, however, you must also consider the drawbacks and risks of starting your own business. There is personal liability, depending on the legal structure of your business and any guarantees you have provided for any business loans. If you can't meet your business liabilities, your creditors can seize your personal property, including your home.

And think hard about how you'll feel without receiving a regular pay cheque, personal benefits, and vacation time with pay. In short, you're on your own with sole responsibility for your business's success. You must have a viable business idea and the skills to make it a success.

Tax savings—two lovely words

It's really important to consult with your tax advisor before starting your business in order to gain a full understanding of the tax implications of your decision. Different kinds of businesses have different classifications and are taxed in different ways. But, as long as you're a sole proprietor, you pay income tax on the profits from the business as part of your personal income tax.

But guess what? You are entitled to deduct all kinds of expenses. Because your home office is part of your home, you may be entitled to claim a percentage of the cost of paying for and maintaining your home. That might include your rent or mortgage interest, your utilities, the part of your phone bill that pertains to business, and some costs associated with preparing your home office. You must have a reasonable expectation of making money before deducting any start-up costs or continuing losses.

You may also be able to deduct some of the cost of running your car if you use your car for business. You get a better deduction if you lease a car than if you buy one. Deductions may include a part of your auto insurance.

If, when you set up your business, you have to buy a desk, computer, fax machine, chair, filing cabinet, software, and cell phone, as well as paper, paper clips, staples, and a desk calendar, save those receipts. The first seven items listed are capital items and can be claimed over several years. The remainder of the items are business expenses and are tax deductible on a current basis. But, you must have bought all of the items for business use.

If you have to take a potential client to lunch to discuss a project, you can pick up the tab and deduct some of the cost of lunch. Remember that all business costs must be reasonable in the circumstances of your business.

So, organize your shoebox and save those receipts!

The upside of downsizing

There are as many reasons why women start their own business as there are businesses, although starting your own business is just a dream until you've got the cash. In some cases, that opportunity presents itself in a strange way.

Many companies are changing their structure and downsizing their staff. When that happens, employees may be given a severance "package." The amount varies depending on a number of factors, including your position, experience, and the number of years you worked for the company.

If you move on to another job very soon after leaving the first one, that package can be a windfall for you to invest in your future. Or, if you've always wanted to start your own business, the funds you receive from your former employer could be the key to that dream.

But be careful. Prepare a realistic budget and determine what you'll need to stay afloat financially while your business is in the start-up phase. It usually takes three to five years to determine whether your business can remain viable.

Most financial institutions offer small business loans to those who qualify. You'll need to prepare a business plan to prove you mean business. You'll have to convince the lender that there's a market for your business and that you're willing to work hard to make it happen. One of the most important criteria will be your ability to repay your loan. Your lender will probably want security in the form of personal assets. This is part of the risk you need to consider when you borrow.

Investing your pension money

Much will change if you leave a company to go out on your own. The biggest change is that you're no longer an employee. That means different things to different people. One thing is for sure: you have to do everything for yourself that your employer used to do for you.

For instance, if you had a pension plan at work, it will terminate once you leave the company. And that means you have some decisions to make.

Some company pension plans are "locked in." That means you can't get your mitts on your money until it's time to retire. If your employer's plan is a locked-in plan and you leave that company, you'll be asked to complete a series of forms that will enable you to move your pension to some other investment company. But a locked-in fund is a locked-in fund and, if you move it, it stays locked in another fund until your retirement.

You may have been saving for retirement with your employer in a savings vehicle that was not locked in. That means you may be handed a chunk of cash when you leave. Think hard. This is your retirement money. Don't blow it. If circumstances force you to cash out your savings, be wise. Plan a way and a time to pay yourself back.

Really safe funds

If risk is a word you don't even want to think about, then segregated funds may be right for you. "Seg funds" allow for the potential for growth on the market, but your original investment is guaranteed. That's because seg funds are considered an insurance product.

Seg funds have certain guarantees. When your deposit matures (usually after a minimum of 10 years), you'll receive the deposit guarantee amount (less the fees) or the market value of the investment, whichever is greater. When you die, your beneficiary will receive the proceeds from your fund. Seg funds may qualify for protection from your creditors even in bankruptcy. That makes them a good investment for business owners who are facing a fairly big business risk.

It's your business

Personal disability insurance takes care of your personal expenses in the event of an accident or a long-term illness. But what if you own your own business and have employees who are counting on you, and creditors waiting to be paid?

If you're a recent business owner, you're likely in the market for business overhead expense insurance.

Personal disability insurance provides an income for you in the event that you are injured or suffer a long-term illness. Business overhead expense insurance provides emergency cash you may need to pay your employees, your rent, or your suppliers. But it doesn't pay you a salary.

So as a prudent entrepreneur, you'll also need both personal and business insurance to look after yourself, your family, and your business.

Starting your own business can be a very exciting, liberating time in your life. It demands a great deal of thought, planning, and discipline to make it work. Keep the faith, believe in yourself, and you'll be successful.

Severance Pay, Inheritance, and the Big Lottery Win

So you're way more wealthy today than you were yesterday. Good for you. Now what?

Windfall money can be a great boost to your retirement savings. It can also be a huge tax problem if you don't think carefully about your new-found money and where you're going to put it.

If you've just been downsized, rightsized, outplaced, or just plain fired, you'll receive some sort of a severance package, also called a retiring allowance. Some people, as we said, use those funds to start a business but, if the idea of being your own boss doesn't appeal to you, and you get another job fairly quickly, you've got a windfall.

Go back to square one of budgeting and use your windfall wisely. You may want to take a vacation or pay down your debt but remember, a retiring allowance, like ordinary employment income, is included in your income. If you get another job with another salary, you could find yourself with a big ugly tax bill in a year that was already stressful enough.

If you don't need to use the funds, you can transfer your "retiring allowance" tax free to an RRSP.

If you don't get another job right away, then your windfall isn't a windfall. It's future income that you'll need if the rejection letters keep rolling in. You could park your money in a money market fund where it will have some growth potential and you can still get your hands on it quickly if you need it. When you do get that job, you may do well to consider more aggressive investments.

Your number came up

If you're one of the lucky few who hit the big lottery jackpot, take a deep breath and do some serious planning. Even better, contact a financial planner, an accountant, and a lawyer to help you to invest wisely. You could probably afford it. It's hard to believe, but reports tell us that many, many lottery winners go on a spending binge after they win and find themselves, just a few years later, without a cent of their winnings left.

Your lottery winnings in Canada are not taxable (but the income you earn on them is subject to tax). Go directly to a financial planner and learn how to manage this great opportunity.

Your rich uncle

Inheritance can be an income you knew about and planned on or, in the case of a rich uncle you never met, a windfall. We do not have an inheritance tax in Canada so your lump-sum inheritance is cash in the bank.

Check your net worth statement and rewrite it. Check your budget and rewrite it. Then check with your financial planner and do something very clever with your new-found wealth.

A taxing situation

It's also important to know that not all saving must involve cutting back on personal expenses. We all pay income tax. And the more you earn, the higher your rate of taxation. But there are ways to reduce your income tax. And refunds are a whole lot more fun than paying. As your financial plan and investment strategies become more complicated, you'll want to take a close look at the income tax implications. Review your tax situation and ensure that you're receiving all the deductions you're entitled to.

Sharpen your pencil

Every taxpayer is allowed certain deductions and credits. If you miss the opportunity to take advantage of them, you might end up paying more money than necessary. Deductions such as RRSP contributions and child care expenses reduce the amount of your taxable income and that means you pay less tax.

If you have investment income in the form of interest, dividends, capital gains, or foreign income, that income is taxable. However, not all income is taxed equally. The amount you pay also depends on whether the funds are held in a registered or non-registered plan.

Take a close look at the information provided by Revenue Canada or contact a tax advisor. Just make sure you don't pay more than your fair share.

Registered plans

Tax is deferred on income from investments you hold in registered plans, such as RRSPs and some pension plans. That income isn't taxable until you actually withdraw your money from the registered plan. At that time, it's taxed as income.

Non-registered plans

Any income you earn from investments held outside registered plans is subject to tax.

Interest is fully taxable at your top marginal tax rate.

Dividends are payments of after-tax profits from a corporation to its shareholders. Dividends from Canadian corporations qualify for the dividend tax credit, which attempts to give you a credit for the tax that has already been paid by the company.

A capital gain or loss is the difference between the price you pay for an investment and the price at which you sell it. If you buy an investment for $100 and sell it for $110, you have a capital gain of $10 or 10 per cent. If you sell the same investment for $90, you have a capital loss of $10 or 10 per cent. Seventy-five per cent of capital gains are taxable. Seventy-five per cent of capital losses can be used to reduce capital gains of the current year or in any of the previous three years, and can be carried forward indefinitely until utilized.

Married?

• As a married couple, look at the tax credits (like charitable and political donations) to which both or either of you are entitled. Make sure the spouse with the higher income uses the tax credit. The more tax credits you use, the lower your tax will be. There is a mechanism for the transferal of unused tax credits of the lower-income spouse to the higher-income spouse.

- If you're married, you can claim a federal tax credit if your spouse makes little or no income.
- You can pay your spouse a reasonable salary for his services to your business.
- Contribute to a spousal RRSP if your spouse is in a lower tax bracket when you plan to withdraw the funds.
- Loan money to the lower-income spouse at the Revenue Canada prescribed rate for investments earning a higher rate of return.
- You can transfer the dividends received from taxable Canadian corporations by the higher-income spouse to the lower-income spouse.
- Apply to share your CPP benefits with your spouse.

Single?

- If you're single, widowed, divorced, or separated and someone in your home depends on your support, your daughter, for example, you may be eligible to claim an "equivalent to married" credit.
- If you're a single parent attending school, you may be entitled to claim a child care expense deduction.

Children?

- The Child Tax Benefit was designed for low- and middle-income families. There is a basic tax benefit for each of your children. You can also claim the cost of child care on your income tax as a deduction. But don't forget to ask the caregiver for a receipt.
- If your children attend private school, check with the school to see whether a portion of the tuition fee is eligible as a tuition fee deduction or a charitable donation.
- If a student attending a post-secondary institution doesn't have sufficient federal tax payable to use the credit, it's transferable to a spouse, a supporting parent, or grandparent. Any unused education credit may be carried forward.
- If you give a cash gift to any of your children over age 18, you enable them to make the maximum deductible contribution to their RRSP, if they have earned income.

Tax Tips for Investors

- Make sure your financial planner informs you of the annual rate of return on your mutual funds, stocks, and bonds on an after-tax basis so you get an accurate picture of the performance of your investments.
- Keep accurate records of the cost base of your assets so you can report accurate capital gains or losses when you redeem your investments.
- Tax shelters are investments intended to provide investors with tax deferral. Be sure to check out the financial risk, the rate of return, the liquidity, and the planner who's advising you to invest. Double check with Revenue Canada to make sure.

Marry well

In our grandparents' day, the term "to marry well" meant to find a rich husband. Today it means to be prepared, be practical, and be happy. You're committing to what you both hope will be a lifelong union. Romance is lovely but practicality is a better bet that you'll both make it work.

Have you both thought about and discussed the following:

- What kind of life do you want? Do you both have the same goals?
- Where do you plan to live?
- What debt do you have? What about your partner?
- Will you share a bank account or keep your own budgets?
- Who pays for what?
- Do you have a will? You may need a new one now.
- Do you approach finances in a similar manner or very differently? How will you resolve the differences in your approaches?

Those parting words

As much as we try and as badly as we wanted it to work out, marriages do break down—and in record numbers. It's a very painful time for everyone, but you must consider the financial implications of ending your marriage.

Before finalizing your divorce, you will probably have a separation time when, as hard as it is, you should try to sort out your finances.

Here are some helpful steps taken by women who went through a separation:

- Opening a personal bank account.
- Cancelling joint credit cards and applying for personal ones.
- Revoking any power of attorney held by the spouse.
- Drafting a new will.
- Listening to Mozart.
- Reading one good book, then another one.

Throughout your separation period and when it comes time to finalize the divorce, you'll want your lawyer and your financial planner involved, particularly if you have children to look after.

You'll need to understand how to divide your assets, including RRSPs and company pension plans, and you'll need to agree on an amount of money that is to provide for the children.

When a marriage doesn't work out, try to keep in mind that old wounds do heal, a new life does begin, and guilt is a wasted emotion. You are not one half of a whole person. You are entire, all by yourself.

Girls just wanna have fun

Life is full of obligations and responsibilities. And sometimes we feel like a pressure cooker about to blow. That's why, in all of your plans, you need to plan on having some fun. Take a vacation. You deserve it. But guess what? You have to plan for that, too.

Think of it this way. Half the fun of a vacation is looking forward to it. If you escape at the last minute and put the whole cost on your credit card, you may have regrets later when it comes time to pay. You may have to plan six months or a year in advance, but it will be worth it to know that the money you spent on your vacation was intended for just that. There are relatively painless ways to plan your getaway.

You can set up a monthly or weekly direct withdrawal plan in a special account, a money market fund, or a Canada Savings Bond. Figure out what kind of vacation you'd like, how much you need to save, and for how long. Mark your calendar in big bold letters: MY HOLIDAY TIME. Think of your saving time as "looking forward to my holiday time."

You can use your line of credit or a credit card if you plan on paying yourself back. But it'll take determination and discipline. And remember, when your holiday's over, you'll still have the debt.

Just before you pack your bags, check out travel insurance. Provincial health plans cover some expenses if you get sick or have an accident while you're away. But many expenses are not covered. Travel insurance, sometimes called out-of-country medical insurance, is relatively inexpensive. Having it can contribute to even greater peace of mind while you're away.

Have a great time!

Financial Health Check-up

To summarize how you're doing so far, keep the following checklist in mind as you measure your progress in getting closer to more balanced financial health.

THE "MAXIMIZING YOUR INVESTMENTS" CHECKLIST

Completion date

- I've checked out my company pension plan and I understand it. _____
- I know which government pension plans are available. _____
- I understand the difference between registered and non-registered plans. _____
- I know how much equity I have in my home. _____
- I have a plan to pay off my mortgage before I retire. _____
- I understand reverse mortgages. _____
- I have calculated how much retirement income I'll need. _____
- I have a plan in place to make sure I have enough money at retirement. _____
- I understand how RRIFs work. _____
- I know about annuities. _____
- I understand what happens when I cash in my RRSP. _____
- I have a will and know about probate fees. _____
- I understand the tax implications of my estate. _____
- I have prearranged my funeral. _____
- I know how my small business can save on taxes. _____
- I understand what segregated funds are. _____
- I know about business disability insurance. _____
- If I come into some surprise money, I know how best to invest it. _____
- I'm taking full advantage of all my tax deductions. _____

- I know how to protect my investments should my marriage break down. _____
- I'm saving for a vacation. _____

Personal Perspectives on the Challenges of Achieving a Richer, More Fulfilling Lifestyle

As you meet the following individuals and understand their personal situations, you may see something of yourself at a certain age or stage of your life.

Following each woman's story are constructive suggestions on how she might deal with the challenges she's facing today. Some of these pointers might also relate to you and your ability to enhance your chance to achieve greater balance and personal fulfillment.

Brittany

Age: 26 (married/two children)
Occupation: Letter Carrier

FINANCIAL SNAPSHOT

Assets		Liabilities	
Car	$6,500	Credit Card Debt	$1,500
RRSPs	$4,000		
Savings	$11,300		
Total Assets:	$21,800	Total Liabilities:	$1,500
Estimated Net Worth:	$20,300		

Estimated Cash Flow
Net Monthly Income $1,850

Key Monthly Expenses

Investment Programs	$40
Household Expenses	$790
Mortgage/Rent	$200
Insurance Plans	$140
Debt Payments	$35
Discretionary Expenses	$600
Total Income	$1,850
Total Expenses	$1,805

Personal snapshot

"I imagined myself as an economist in a bank. In fact, I was halfway to a degree when I met my husband Paul and we got married. A year later, I had the twins, Samantha and Jonathan. It was quite a change for me to move into this little house on the outskirts of Saskatoon and look for a job that would give me time to care for the children. I've changed my goals—but I love my life.

"I analyzed all of the part-time job possibilities and I settled on the post office. First, I thought walking would be great exercise so I applied to be a "casual" letter carrier, which gives me a good 2.5-hour walk when I'm working. I'm paid well for a part-timer, $18 an hour, and I average about 28 hours a week. It gives me time to take care of the children and also take a correspondence course with the local agricultural college. I'm learning how to run a modern farm. My economics background is really kicking in because farming is less about cows and more about marketing. My parents own a farm located an hour away from here, and they plan to leave it to me. Paul, who's an independent carpenter, likes the idea as much as I do.

"When we married, we both made wills in each others' favour and we designated my parents as the kids' guardians. Paul immediately took out life and disability insurance, which he says is his form of saving. Then sadly, Paul's Mom passed away, and left him $9,000. My instinct was to save it all. I felt I knew everything about developing a financial plan. But Paul said we should run it by an advisor at our bank. He was right.

"My field was macroeconomics; I turned out not to be so sound on micro. It wasn't until we were sitting down with the advisor that I realized Paul and I had been less than a partnership. I tend to be the idea person and Paul has gone along so far. But now—for the first time—we were able to sit down and discuss our short- and long-term goals and we found out that we had differences. For example, Paul wanted us to buy the house we live in. It's up for sale right now. We could afford the down payment with Paul's recent inheritance and we'd pay less per month on a mortgage than we now pay for rent. Paul emphasized it would increase our net worth if we invest the difference between our rent and mortgage payments, and given the good area we're in, we'd likely make some money when we sold.

"It's funny how I reacted to that. I wanted to stash it all in savings and keep it for a rainy day. But the advisor came down on Paul's side. I realized that I was being rather selfish. I was willing to defer a house until we moved into my parents' house, which, of course, I love. But as Paul pointed out, that might not happen for 10 years. In the meantime, why shouldn't we have a nice house to live in if it makes financial sense to do so? He was right. That day I learned compromise.

"I'm a little superstitious. We're doing so well and we're so happy, and I feel we've got a great future. We don't have much social life because of the twins and the cost of babysitting, but we do what we can with pot-luck suppers and barbecues with other parents. I guess you could say we're deferring our fun until later on."

FQ rating: A

Considerations: Great going, Brittany. You've got everything in balance. Your family is clearly the priority at the moment, you're keeping fit, you're staying in touch with others, and you have the courage to know what you want and you're going after it.

I get really encouraged when I run into someone like you who enjoys building toward financial security. I'm finding that more and more women are becoming enthusiastic participants in financial planning for their future rather than leaving it to their husbands or partners. What's most impressive is the way you and Paul are now working together, that you're able to discuss everything openly, and that you're able to compromise. I tend to think that teamwork is essential to keep a financial plan on track.

I have just a couple of questions. I see Paul has life and disability insurance but what if something were to happen to you? Are you covered adequately? I really hope you'll more fully explore the benefits of an RRSP. You may find you have enough saved for your children's education now and can let time and compounding work for you if you used some of those saved dollars to maximize both your RRSP contributions.

Kay

Age:	49 (partner/no children)
Occupation:	Career Business Consultant

FINANCIAL SNAPSHOT

Assets		Liabilities	
Car	$6,000	Credit Card Debt	$1,350
Savings	$40,100		
RRSPs	$50,000		
Investments	$30,000		
Life Insurance	$60,000		
Total Assets:	$186,100	Total Liabilities:	$1,350
Estimated Net Worth:	$184,750		

Estimated Cash Flow

Net Monthly Income	$2,600

Key Monthly Expenses

Investment Programs	$235

Household Expenses	$600
Mortgage/Rent	$800
Insurance Plans	$180
Debt Payments	$250
Discretionary Expenses	$250
Total Income	$2,600
Total Expenses	$2,315

Personal snapshot

"I'm a 'saver' in partnership with an 'adventurer.' It's a great partnership even though we're so different. I've been saving since I was 20 when I was working my way through college. My dad drilled it into me. I was an only child and had to rely on myself. I have a marketing degree and I was well established in a top corporation when I met Mark, my partner. He was in marketing too, but he was restless. He made it clear that he wanted to keep moving, which might mean living in different cities, different countries.

"I was on the fast track in my firm, a woman who was considered promotable, or that's what my boss told me. Linking up with Mark meant that I would have to give up all that. My dad had a fit! But I wrote down all the pluses and minuses of having a career or living with Mark, and I decided on Mark. I believed in myself and felt my skills were transferable to another job and another company. So far, I've been right.

"Here's what our life's like. Ten years ago, Mark decided to leave his job and go to the wine college in Australia. He wanted to become a wine agent. I had no trouble getting a good job in the marketing department of a big winemaker. We had a great time for five wonderful years. When we came home, Mark opened his own wine agency. I am working for a big international consulting firm. I have also set up my own company, which Mark pays for consulting, marketing, and accounting services. When Mark took a business trip to Italy last year, I learned Italian (the lessons were tax-deductible) and I went along as a paid interpreter. We rent an apartment rather than own a house. I don't want the hassle of renting a house when we go away. Mark pays more for the apartment because he uses it as his full-time office; otherwise we share all household expenses.

"I stick to a budget, Mark doesn't. Mark has no RRSPs, but I put the maximum amount allowed into RRSPs every year. I have a couple of credit cards and I pay off the balance each month. I have had life insurance since I was 21, and I have an investment portfolio handled by my bank. But I approve all transactions. I have balanced high risk with steady growth. I like to think I control money and that it doesn't control me.

"At the moment, I could retire and live just the way I do now—comfortably. I'm healthy and I swim five days a week. It's the only kind of exercise that I can bear. I picked up the habit in Australia. I know that circumstances can change, I can change, my lifestyle can change, so I'm thinking about being a little more conservative about my investments. Time to think seriously about retirement, I guess."

FQ rating: A

Considerations: I like your style, Kay, and the way you've really made yourself independent without letting that admirable independence affect your relationship. I'm seeing more and more women like you, thank goodness, who are able to do this. You've feathered your nest nicely. I just have a couple of questions.

It appears you have a relatively substantial amount of uncommitted monthly income—money left over after paying your monthly expenses—which might be put to very good use through some kind of retirement plan. Your savings account is also quite healthy, which begs the question of whether it's invested in the most appropriate manner. With what you have at your disposal for investment purposes, I strongly suggest that you investigate the appropriate asset allocation strategies that a professional investment advisor would recommend. Take advantage of the people and financial products that can help you to invest wisely.

I'm surprised there's no indication of medical insurance expenditures when you travel or live abroad. I can't overemphasize how essential it is that you're protected for any eventuality when you're out of the country. Travel insurance is as easy as a phone call, a click on the Web, or a chat at the bank. As they say, don't leave home without it.

I'm also interested to know if you've investigated whether you're better off renting than owning. Your point about how troublesome it can be to rent a house while you're away is understandable. Still, it might be worth owning for the longer-term potential value of real estate despite the current tax advantages to Mark. Keep in mind that when you sell your principal residence, you don't have to pay capital gains tax. Incidentally, you indicated you have life insurance—does Mark?

Mary

Age: 31 (single mother, one child)
Occupation: Administrative Assistant

FINANCIAL SNAPSHOT

Assets		*Liabilities*	
RRSPs	$4,000	Credit Card Debt	$800
Savings	$1,700		
Inheritance	$18,000		
Total Assets:	$23,700	Total Liabilities:	$800

Estimated Net Worth: $22,900

Estimated Cash Flow
Net Monthly Income $1,900

Key Monthly Expenses

Investment Programs	$60
Household Expenses	$960
Mortgage/Rent	$200
Insurance Plans	$100
Debt Payments	$300
Discretionary Expenses	$190

Total Income	$1,900
Total Expenses	$1,810

Personal snapshot

"I'm a single mom with a four-year-old son and, lucky for me, I have a break on housing. The parents of Robby's father own a little house downtown and they're renting it to me for a lot less than they'd get from anyone who wasn't family. Gramps told me it's just enough to cover the taxes on the place.

"Before I had Robby, I was little Ms. Ambition. I zipped through university, took a liberal arts degree, and immediately got my feet on the corporate ladder with a big public relations firm. I had a knack. I was going places. Then I met Peter. All I can say is that I found myself pregnant and decided to have Robby. Peter took off.

"Robby is worth everything. And though I've had to put my dreams of a demanding career on hold, I don't mind. It's been a challenge to find a steady job with regular hours—one that will allow me to bring Robby into work if I'm stuck—but I've found it and my boss is great.

"I contributed to my former employer's Group RRSP. Today I am absolutely determined to save $60 a month and I do. I need a car and after analyzing my options, I decided on leasing. I qualify for a subsidy for most of Robby's day care but I still have to find $200 a month. I have freebies: I work out at the local community centre and I've joined a free jogging club in the nearby park. I grow vegetables in my backyard and freeze them in the freezer my mom gave me.

"I shop only at discount stores, even for clothes. It's so cool—my mom and I are the same size so I can borrow her classy clothes when I need to. I have a new boyfriend who lives in New York. We exchange visits every month. That's kind of why my credit card balance is off the screen. I'm just able to keep up with the payments.

"Something sad happened: my grandma died. She was the best. I was shocked when my dad told me she'd left me $18,000. There were strings attached, however. I had to save at least half of it for Robby. It is a miracle. A weight's lifted off me. Now I know Robby's going to be all right.

I just want to go out and spend the rest!"

FQ rating: A

Considerations: How about considering a controlled splurge with your new windfall? You could take a small sum and spend it any way you like. Let's face it, Mary, you've learned a lesson about just how hard life can be for a single mother. What's impressive is that you haven't let it get you down. You're keeping fit, you have a new boyfriend, you're certainly not shortchanging Robby, and you haven't lost your spirit. Plus you have a regular savings plan.

It seems to me that your grandmother may have had something like an education savings plan or an in-trust account in mind for Robby. I don't think much of anything happens purely by coincidence, so I encourage you to investigate how a good portion of that money could be invested on Robby's behalf. Registered education savings plans are the logical place to start and you could look into them at your bank.

At the same time, explore the possibility of an informal trust, which would be set up in his name and used for virtually any future need. There are pros and cons to all such plans, so discuss your options when you talk to an expert. But do it!

At the same time—and given your independence and Robby's dependency on you—I think you should consider both life and disability insurance plans. You can get an idea of the rates from the Internet, at a bank, or from a professional advisor. Some companies offer instant assessments on-line. Further, have you made a will in Robby's favour or considered who should be Robby's guardian if anything happened to you?

I certainly won't be the only person to tell you that your primary objective must be to get rid of your credit card debt. Those payments are a growing burden. Once done, you have all sorts of options. What about contributing more to RRSPs and using the tax refund for some discretionary items? You might want to invest more in an education savings plan for Robby or firm up your emergency fund. You have the capital— that is, the cash—to get a head start on a very prudent investment portfolio.

Michelle

Age:	47 (married/two children)
Occupation:	Stay-at-home Mom

FINANCIAL SNAPSHOT

Assets		Liabilities	
Car	$4,500	nil	
Savings	$12,000		
RRSPs	$50,000		
Bonds	$1,500		
Total Assets:	$68,000	Total Liabilities:	nil

Estimated Net Worth:	$68,000

Estimated Cash Flow

Net Monthly Income	$3,000

Key Monthly Expenses

Household Expenses	$3,000
Total Income	$3,000
Total Expenses	$3,000

Personal snapshot

"My husband Kevin, who's closing in on 50, and I are having the time of our lives. Then the other day, we sat down and realized that we had to start saving fast if we were to have anything like as good a life when we retire as we do now. I panicked.

"I can't believe it. Here I am, happily married with two great kids—Cathy who is nine and Paul who's just six—we have a gorgeous house, I have time to spend at least a day on the golf course. We're able to go to the cottage every summer.

"My responsibility is the household and raising the kids, and Kevin gives me $3,000 for hydro, gas, food and house maintenance, and to buy what the children need. It's more than enough, I think. When I want to buy something for myself, I just cash in a Canada Savings Bond. I've been buying bonds since I was in my twenties and using them as mad money.

"I have $50,000 in RRSPs that my financial advisor—yes I've had one for years—has put into mutual funds. And I'm on top of my investments too. A few years ago, I picked a European growth fund that has done very nicely. The rest of my portfolio has not done as well, but I understand the Canadian market hasn't performed like others. Still, I really wonder if I should be making better investments. I don't buy lottery tickets because the odds scare me, but I love playing blackjack when I get the chance. If I won say, a million dollars, I'd go around the world—and only then pay off the mortgage and debts.

"Until I married 10 years ago, I was entirely self-supporting. I trained to be a teacher, then moved into business. By the time I was 34, I was heading up the in-house education unit of a major corporation and earning $58,000 a year. The company matched my RRSP contributions and when I left to get married, they were locked in. I thought I was never going back. But I had to.

"Right after Cathy was born Kevin hit a bad patch. He's in advertising and things go up and down. Anyway, I was lucky to get a part-time contract with my old company and I earned around $34,000 a year. Then Kevin got a new project and a big promotion, and we decided I could give up work and stay home. Hooray!

"We both own the house and we both have made wills. Kevin's taken out life insurance for both of us. If I die, he can bury me, and if he dies, I can pay off the mortgage. Kevin's also started contributing to a registered education savings plan for the children's education. But we still can't budget properly. I just don't know where the money goes."

FQ rating: A

Considerations: Despite the fact that you say you're panicking, I think you're doing pretty well in most departments. You're the generation of Boomer Moms. You had a successful career before you married and you had your family comparatively late. This makes home life all the more satisfying.

I've met many women like you—reluctant to pick up their career once they've discovered the joys of motherhood. For the first time in their lives, they're relaxed; like you, they're also fit. The idea of getting back into outside employment isn't very appealing.

You say you have a financial advisor for your investments. I think you would do well to expand her role and ask her to draw up a financial plan for you with more emphasis on your retirement needs. Of course, Kevin would have to be part of this because the plan should take into account the family's entire financial details.

I'm a little puzzled by your insurance arrangements and actually think you should both consult with an insurance specialist. You have a $3,000 monthly budget and it might be helpful for you to have a family cash-flow plan done—a stricter budget!—so you know exactly where the money is going. You might find there's more room for savings. At the very least, you'll gain greater control over your money.

For your personal peace of mind, I believe you should be more aware of the total picture, and perhaps you are. But the $3,000 you have to "manage the household," is that to cover family emergencies too? It's clearly not enough to cover your own personal "mad money" needs if you're cashing the occasional Canada Savings Bond. What happens when they run out?

In Closing

Life is a series of learning opportunities. Vibrant, healthy people keep their minds open to new information every day of their life. That applies to everything—family, friends, fitness, finances, and focus. Keep learning and keep growing. It is your future. Make the most of it.

Index

A

active manager, 65
amortization period, 40
annual rate of return, 115
annuity, 99–100
anticipated return, 58
asset classes, 57
asset cost base, 115
asset management programs, 67
auto insurance, 37
automatic withdrawals, 29

B

back-end load, 66
balanced funds, 62
balanced portfolio, 58
bank accounts, 58
bankers, 64
bankers' acceptances, 57
bear market, 68
budget, 21, 24–25
bull market, 68
business overhead expense
  insurance, 110

C

Canada Education Savings Grant
  (CESG), 77
Canada Mortgage and Housing
Corporation (CMHC), 40
Canada Pension Plan, 11, 95
car insurance, 37
cash in/outflow worksheet, 22
cash value of insurance policy, 33
cash-flow problems, 9–10
Certified Financial Planner
  (CFP), 74
charitable gifts, 105–6
Chartered Financial Analyst
  (CFA), 74
codicil, 103
commercial paper, 57
commission, 75
compound interest, 7
compounding, 29, 69
consolidation loan, 9, 27, 71
conventional mortgage, 40
conventional will, 102–3
corporate bonds, 56, 57
co-signer, 25
credit card debt, 8–9
credit rating, 25

D

death benefits, 106
debt, 25–26
debt securities, 56, 57
debt/service ratio, 38, 71

defined benefit plan, 94
defined contribution plan, 94–95
direct withdrawal savings, 29
disability insurance, 34–35, 110
disposable income, 25
diversification, 61, 63–64, 68–69
dollar cost averaging, 69
double up on payments, 41
Dow Jones Industrial Average, 59

E
economic cycle, 63
eligible investments, 30
emergency fund, 28, 54
employer pension plans, 11,
  94–95, 109–10
equity funds, 62, 63
equity in home, 96
equity market, 57
equity securities, 56
estate planning, 100–101
executor, 103
expenses, 24

F
family cash-flow plan, 130
financial advisors. *See* financial
  planners
financial plan, 20, 84, 130
financial planners, 12, 51, 64, 74,
  96–97
fixed-income investments, 58–59
fixed-income market, 57
foreign investments, 69

formal will, 102–3
front-end load, 66
fund managers, 65
funeral costs, 104–5

G
GE Capital, 40
GICs, 58
global mutual funds, 62, 69
goals, 20–21
government bonds, 56, 57
government pension plans, 95–96
gross monthly income, 38
group insurance, 34
group RRSPs, 72–73
growth funds, 62
growth investments, 58, 59
guaranteed annuities, 100
guaranteed insurability, 79

H
hedging, 68
high-interest-rate economy, 63
high-ratio mortgage, 40
holograph will, 103
Home Buyers' Plan, 39
home insurance, 36
Human Resources Development
  Canada, 96

I
income funds, 62
income investments, 58
income splitting, 72, 86

income tax
  attribution rules, 105
  capital gains, 102, 113, 125
  cashing-in RRSPs, 100
  charitable gifts, 105–6
  Child Tax Benefit, 114
  death and, 101–2
  deductions, 108, 113
  deemed disposition, 106
  dividend income, 113, 114
  donation tax credit, 106
  foreign income, 113
  foreign property, 102
  income splitting, 72, 86
  interest income, 113
  investment income, 113
  non-registered plans, 113
  paying, 11
  reducing, 112–15
  registered plans, 113
  RRSP contributions, 30, 73
  and self-employment, 107–8
  student loan interest tax credit, 89
  tax credits, 114
index, 59
index funds, 62, 65–66
indexed annuities, 100
inflation, 63
informal trust. See in-trust account
inheritances, 112
interest rates, 40
in-trust account, 78, 127

irregular expenses, 24

L
life insurance, 31–32, 33–34, 78–79, 106
lifetime annuities, 99–100
living wills, 104
loans, 25
locked-in pension plans, 109–10
long-term investment, 69
lottery winnings, 112

M
management expense ratio, 66
market performance, 59
money market, 57
money market mutual funds, 58, 62
money purchase plan, 94–95
mortgage interest rates, 40
mortgage payments, 41
mortgage renewal, 40–41
mortgage term, 40
mortgage-backed securities, 57
mutual funds, 60
  active manager, 65
  affordability, 60–61
  annual rate of return, 115
  back-end load, 66
  balanced funds, 62
  convenience, 60
  diversification, 61
  equity funds, 62, 63
  flexibility, 61

front-end load, 66

global funds, 62, 69

growth funds, 62

income funds, 62

index funds, 62, 65–66

management expense ratio, 66

management fee, 65–66

management style, 65

money market, 58, 62

net asset value, 65

no-load funds, 66

on-line, 80

operating expenses, 66

passive managers, 65

performance, 63

professional management, 60

RRSP-eligibility, 61

selecting, 64

track record, 66–67

N

NASDAQ, 57

net worth, 21

net worth statement, 21

New York Stock Exchange, 57

no-load funds, 66

notorial will, 103

O

Old Age Security, 96

out-of-country medical insurance, 117, 125

owners' liability coverage, 36

P

passive managers, 65

pay yourself first, 6, 23, 27

pension plans. *See* employer pension plans; government pension
plans; locked-in pension plans

permanent insurance, 33

Personal Financial Planner (PFP),
74

personal line of credit, 28

PIT, 41

power of attorney, 103–4

pre-approved mortgage, 38

pre-authorized purchase plan, 79

pre-payment of mortgage principal, 41

principal and interest, 41

principal residence, 125

probate fees, 101

property taxes, 41

provincial health plans, 117

Q

Quebec Pension Plan, 95

R

rebalancing, 67–68

recovering economy, 63

Registered Education Savings
Plan. *See* RESP

Registered Retirement Income
Fund (RRIF), 99

Registered Retirement Savings
Plan. *See* RRSPs

renewal of mortgage, 40–41

RESP, 51, 77–78, 127

retirement savings, 7

retiring allowance, 111–12

right of survivorship, 105

risk level, 58, 63–64

risk management, 84

risk/return trade-off, 58, 68

RRIF, 99

RRSPs, 30
   age 69 rollover, 98
   beneficiary, 101, 105
   borrowing for, 71
   cashing-in, 10, 100
   contribution limits, 70–71
   contributions, 30
   and death, 101
   deductibility of contributions, 30, 73
   downpayment on home purchase, 39
   eligible investments, 30, 58, 61
   foreign investments, 69–70
   group, 72–73
   maximization of contributions, 70, 84
   reasons for buying, 30–31
   spousal, 71–72, 114
   transition rules, 98

S

S&P 500 Stock Price Index, 59–60

safety-class investments, 57, 58

savings, 10, 23–24, 27, 28–29

segregated funds, 110

severance pay, 111–12

short-term debt securities, 57

short-term GICs, 58

simplified prospectus, 66

spending, 22–23

spousal RRSPs, 71–72, 114

Standard & Poor's 500 Stock Price index, 59–60

stock market, 57

stocks, 56, 59

T

T-bill, 56

tax shelters, 115

term annuities, 99

term deposits, 58

term insurance, 32–33

term to 100 insurance, 33

Toronto Stock Exchange, 57, 59

travel insurance, 117, 125

Treasury bills, 56, 57

TSE 300 Composite Index, 59

U

universal life insurance, 33

V

volatility, 63

W

whole life insurance, 33

wills, 102–4